Leading from Within:
Shifting Persepctives on Leadership

– VONGAI NYAHUNZVI –

An environmentally friendly book printed and bound in England by
www.printondemand-worldwide.com

http://www.fast-print.net/bookshop

LEADING FROM WITHIN:
SHIFTING PERSPECTIVES ON LEADERSHIP
Copyright © Vongai Nyahunzvi 2016

A catalogue record for this book is available from the British Library

ISBN 978-178456-318-9

First published 2016 by
FASTPRINT PUBLISHING
Peterborough, England.

Contents

Acknowledgements

I dedicate this book to my husband and best friend, Studymore Nyahunzvi, and my children, Myles and Ethan Nyahunzvi, who have always been a dependable source of encouragement to me.

To my parents John and Viola Chimbambo for educating and believing in me, and my siblings, who cheered me on all the way.

I would also like to thank all my friends and family who have directly or indirectly contributed to this book.

Foreword

There are many ways to finish the sentence "leadership is…". Many of us intuitively know what leadership means but it can have different meanings for different people. As soon as we try to define leadership, we immediately discover it has many different forms.

Leadership can be defined in terms of the power relationships that exist between a leader and their followers. It can also be a process for helping others achieve goals. Some address leadership from a skills perspective.

A quick Google search for 'leadership books' returns close to 300,000 results. This includes all aspects of leadership, from listings of the 'best leadership books ever written' to the top 15 books for young leaders, to books on specific types of leadership roles in businesses and organisations. In addition to popular books, there are many publications about leadership in research literature, including scholarly studies on theoretical approaches to explain the complexities of leadership — traits, behaviour, qualifications, process, personality, etc.

Collectively, findings on leadership provide a picture of a process that is far more sophisticated and complex than the view presented in some popular books. This is a different leadership book. This offers a unique perspective on leadership — leading from within.

This book is about your own personal leadership development, not about leadership within structures — organisational or social — or corporate hierarchy. The shifting perspective on leadership found here centres on putting your ego aside for the greater reward of finding fulfilment in the impact you have in your life and the lives of others. The material is presented in a clear, concise and interesting manner.

You will also find several other features to make it more user friendly:

- Each chapter follows the same format and is structured to include notable leadership quotes, descriptions and discussions of the chapter topic, the point in action and reflection questions.
- Each chapter includes an interpretation of theory first, then practice.
- Each chapter includes an application section that discusses the practical aspects of the theory and how it can be used effectively.
- Leadership instruments and tools are suggested throughout.

Through these special features, we have made every effort to ensure this book is substantive, easy to understand and practical.

Dr Kerry Mitchell-Jones
PhD, MBA

Preface

This book is for individuals who want to make a difference and leave a positive legacy. I believe very strongly that everyone was born to lead in one way or another: you might lead just yourself or one other person; you might lead a handful or hundreds of people; you might even be destined to lead nations. You might not be in charge, you might not have any formal authority, you might be fettered by a dozen limitations, but if you really want to lead, you can. You can make a difference in the world through leadership and express its qualities in whatever context you are in.

Not everyone is meant to be a company CEO or executive, but that should not stop you from being a leader. Follow the wisdom of your heart and mind; set a trail that is only revealed as you courageously walk along it. This is what I call leading from within and is what I deeply believe in.

There are millions of books, articles, studies and reviews on leadership, but what fascinates me is that it seems no one has cracked it. Most books emphasise the external manifestations of leadership such as drive, charisma and vision, to name a few. The underlying assumption is that leadership is what we do to other people. But, according to Edgar Schein (leadership expert and author of *Organisational Culture and Leadership*), leadership is something we do **with** other people.

When I talk about leadership in this book, I am **not** talking about:

- seniority or your position in an organisation;
- titles — you don't need a title to lead; or
- personal attributes — say the word 'leader' and most people think of a domineering, take-charge, charismatic individual.

> *Leadership is a decision, not a position*

Given the complex environment that leaders operate in, I strongly believe that how they are perceived, handle relationships and work with systems are critical ingredients for success.

Section 1: Leading from Within

"Your visions will become clear only when you can look into your own heart. Who looks outside, dreams; who looks inside, awakes." **C G Jung**

"The more self-aware an animal is, the more empathetic it tends to be." **Frans de Waal**

My passion to explore leading from within started 10 years ago, after a challenge from my then mentor, who suggested I explore who I was and why I did what I did. She told me to think about how much of my leadership comes from within and look for evidence of it.

This profound challenge shocked my world in ways I did not expect. Until that point, I had so much pride in what I had achieved. I had been on a career trajectory that gave me my first head of department job at 26 and saw me working at director level by the time I was 29: I felt I was an example of 'good' leadership and had it cracked. I had also studied a number of programmes and qualifications on leadership development and self-awareness, and had taught and worked on several leadership development programmes.

This was the beginning of my hunger to learn and explore what it means to lead from within. I have come to appreciate that it doesn't matter what the external manifestation of leadership is; if you don't start with your unique values and beliefs and lead with inner congruence, you might not be working at your full capacity or individual potential, regardless of your position or rank.

I like what Erica Fox (author of *Winning from within: a breakthrough method for leading, living and lasting change, (2013)* said: "It's not possible to be a visionary leader if you do not have the ability to connect to the vision that lies within you, cultivate it, and share it with others."

In this book I share the truths I found useful on my search for what it means to lead from within. You will gain insights that empower you to make wise decisions and act with a deeper understanding and knowledge of yourself. Once you are tuned into it, this kind of leadership flows easily. It's not forced, aggressive or controlling. If you follow them, the principles in this book will produce positive results that help you balance your relationships, both personally and professionally. You will begin to easily attract people and the resources you need to lead and live a fun and fulfilling life.

I begin by exploring self-awareness and suggesting ways to heighten it, such as seeking feedback, acknowledging your blind spots, establishing your growth edges and understanding your personality preferences. Section 2 explores leading through others, and Section 3 looks at leading with others in a complex environment.

Chapter 1: Self-awareness

"When I discover who I am, I'll be free."
Ralph Ellison

"You can't get away from yourself.
You can't decide not to see yourself anymore.
You can't decide to turn off the noise in your head."
Jay Asher

What Is Self-Awareness?

Before you can lead others, you have to be able to lead yourself. To do that, you need to know yourself. Developing self-awareness is a critical aspect of your leadership journey. Self-awareness is the capacity for introspection and the ability to recognise yourself as an individual. It allows you to understand other people and see how they perceive you, your attitude and your responses to them from moment to moment.

In their research on self-awareness, Professor Thomas Hills et al. (2014) of Warwick University's psychology department highlighted that most of us think we know and are leading ourselves when, in fact, we are not. This occurs because of a fundamental misunderstanding of who we are. Many leadership programmes lead people 'fundamentally' astray because they build on this basic misunderstanding, instead of stripping it away. That's why many of our current ideas about leadership are not only incorrect, they are destructive — and many of our leaders today exhibit both destructive and self-destructive qualities.

Why Develop Self-Awareness?

According to a study conducted by Green Peak Partners (2010), there is a strong correlation between leadership success and high scores of self-awareness. Self-awareness — a clear understanding of your personality and how others perceive you — is an essential tool for successful leadership, and a trait all good managers should strive for.

Self-awareness is the first step in creating what you want and mastering 'you'. Focusing your attention, emotions, reactions, personality and behaviour determines where you go in life. As you develop self-awareness, you are able to change your thoughts and interpretations. Changing your interpretations allows you to change your emotions.

Having self-awareness allows you to see where your thoughts and emotions are taking you. It also helps you to see what controls your emotions, behaviour and personality, so you can make the changes you want. Until you are aware (in the moment) of what controls your thoughts, emotions, words and behaviour, it will be difficult to change the direction of your life.

At an interpersonal level, self-awareness of your strengths and weaknesses can gain you the trust of others and increase your credibility, both of which will increase your leadership effectiveness. At an organisational level, the benefits are even greater. When you acknowledge what you have yet to learn, you model that in your organisation and say it's okay if you don't have all the answers, make mistakes and, most importantly, need to ask for help. These are all characteristics of an organisation that is constantly learning and spring-boarding innovation and agility, two hallmarks of high-performing organisations.

Loretta Malandro, author of *Fearless Leadership (2009),* highlighted the importance of self-awareness: "Over the years, I've worked with leaders or been led by leaders who end up derailing their careers or reputation due to lack of self-awareness. These individuals believed that they were omnipotent and took crazy risks or didn't recognise when actions that felt authoritative were actually demoralising or in general didn't have an accurate "read" on how others were decoding the messages they were sending."

Self-awareness is not just about your good side, it's also about your shortcomings. Leaders who are aware of their strengths and shortcomings are seen as authentic and people gravitate towards them.

In his book, *Five levels of being* (2014), Schumacher highlighted that in their pursuit of self-awareness, human beings confront four questions:

1. What is really going on in my own inner world?
2. What is going on in the inner world of other beings?
3. What do I look like in the eyes of other beings?
4. What do I actually observe in the world around me?

Types Of Self-Awareness

In their book *Essential social psychology* (2010), psychologists Crisp and Turner identified three types of awareness:

> *Self-awareness is the capacity for introspection and the ability to recognise yourself as an individual, separate from the environment and from others*

Public self-awareness emerges when people are aware of how they appear to others. It often shows when someone is the centre of attention, such as giving a presentation or talking to a group of friends. This type of self-awareness often compels people to adhere to social norms. When we are aware we are being watched and evaluated, we often try to behave in ways that are more socially acceptable and desirable. Public self-awareness can also lead to evaluation anxiety, when people become distressed, anxious, or worried about how others see them.

Private self-awareness happens when people become aware of some aspects of themselves, but only in a private way. For example, seeing your face in the mirror is a type of private self-awareness. Feeling your stomach lurch when you realise you forgot to write an important report or feeling your heart flutter when you see someone you are attracted to are also good examples.

Self-consciousness is a heightened state of self-awareness. Sometimes, people can become overly self-aware and veer into what is known as self-consciousness. Have you ever felt like everyone was watching you, judging your actions and waiting to see what you would do next? This heightened state of self-awareness can leave you feeling awkward and nervous. In many cases, these feelings of self-consciousness are only temporary and arise in situations when we are in the spotlight. For some people, self-consciousness can become a chronic condition. People who are privately self-conscious have a higher level of private self-awareness, which can be both good and bad. These individuals tend to be more aware of their feelings and beliefs, and so are more likely to stick to their personal values. However, they are also more likely to suffer from negative health consequences such as increased stress and anxiety.

Point In Action

There are many examples of leaders demonstrating high levels of self-awareness and an equal number showing a lack of it. A positive example is the US President, Barack Obama. He has been praised for many things: his soaring speech, his cool and calm demeanour, his comedic timing. What I like most is his high level of self-awareness, especially on his shortcomings.

After a disastrous debate against Governor Mitt Romney, Obama's whole 2008 campaign was in crisis. The worst part was that he looked dis-pirited and unsure. Here is Obama reacting to his campaign manager's frantic pleas to change his debate style, from the book *Double Down*.

"Last night wasn't good, and I know that. Here's why I think I'm having trouble. I'm having a hard time squaring up what I know I need to do, what you guys are telling me I need to do, with where my mind takes me, which is: I'm a lawyer, and I want to argue things out. I want to peel back layers.

It's against my instincts just to perform. It's easy for me to slip back into what I know, which is basically to dissect arguments. I think when I talk. It can be halting. I start slow. It's hard for me to just go into my answer. I'm having to teach my brain to function differently.

I can't tell you that 'okay, I woke up today, I knew I needed to do better, and I'll do better'. I am wired in a different way than this event requires. I just don't know if I can do this."

This proved to be a cataclysmic moment for the campaign. There was still work ahead for him, but by acknowledging his failure and his fears, Obama was better equipped to do something about it. He had defined the problem.

> *Being aware of your flaws and that you need to work on them will help you become a better leader*

Understanding your flaws doesn't mean you accept them and do nothing else. It means you are aware they are there, and that you need to work on them to become a better leader. Surprisingly, many leaders cannot accept their deficiencies in the first place.

Ways To Cultivate And Develop Self-Awareness

Developing self-awareness is a process, not an event. It comes through focusing your attention on the details of your personality and behaviour. It is not learnt just from reading a book. When you do that, you focus your attention on conceptual ideas. With your attention on a book you are not paying attention to your own behaviour, emotions and personality.

There are a number of ways you can develop and increase your awareness of self:

1. **Seek feedback.** As a leader, it's crucial for you to have an insight into how you are perceived. Ask your colleagues to participate in 360-degree feedback, where your subordinates, peers and supervisors provide anonymous opinions on your strengths and areas for improvement. You can also use less formal channels. Ask people you work with for feedback after you have completed specific projects. Remember to ask direct questions, listen attentively and don't justify or defend your actions. Asking for feedback creates an overall sense of accountability and encourages a practice of honest communication. We will talk more about feedback in the next chapter.

2. **Acknowledge your blind spots**. Become intimate not just with your strengths but also your blind spots, those aspects of your personality that can derail you. John C. Maxwell, author of *Developing the leader within you* (2012), defines a blind spot as "an area in the lives of people in which they continually do not see themselves or their situation realistically." We will look at this in more detail in next chapter.

3. **Use tools for understanding yourself.** There are many psychometric tools to help you assess your strengths and areas for development. While these tests won't provide an exhaustive description of your personality, they can be effective tools for

recognising how you interact with other people, what motivates your decision making, and how you approach problems. There a more details in Chapter 3.

4. **Create tangible tools for self-reflection.** Many successful leaders record important decisions and reflect on them later. Create a habit of writing down key decisions and the motivations that influenced them. After six months or a year, re-examine those decisions to see whether your assumptions were accurate or misguided (this can be undertaken privately or formally, with others). This process can help avoid the trap of repeating mistakes.

5. **Admit mistakes.** It might be a cliché, but effective leaders know that admitting a mistake is a sign of strength, not weakness. It damages your credibility most when you ignore mistakes or allow blame to fall on someone else's shoulders. Taking responsibility for your actions and apologising when you've made a mistake demonstrates the value you place on openness and accountability. Looking at the case above, Obama admitting his mistakes and limitations was one of the critical reasons people warmed to him.

6. **Keep an open mind.** When you have the ability to regulate your own emotional world, you can be attuned to the emotions of others. To be a successful leader, you have to be curious about new people and all they have to offer. This shows that you can be a team player who doesn't necessarily need to be

'number one'. The more open you are to others, the more creative you become.

Reflection Questions

1. Personal: Who are you? What are your personal strengths and weaknesses? What are your core beliefs? What are your fears and dreams?
2. Social: Who are you in public? Who are you around other people? What kind of impression do you try to make? What kind of people do you like to hang out with?
3. Work: What is your calling? What kind of work do you enjoy? What activities make you happy?
4. How do you feel under pressure?
5. When someone criticises you at work, how does that make you feel? What narrative do you tell yourself?
6. Under what circumstances do you open yourself to others?
7. What kind of support do you need more of in your life?

Chapter 2:
Knowing your Purpose

"When a man does not know what harbour
he is making for, no wind is the right wind."
Seneca

"Having a purpose is the difference between
making a living and making a life."
Tom Thiss

Knowing and living your life purpose is the most crucial step forward in your development path. When you are 'living on purpose', your problems tend to fly out the window. And yet most leaders are not able to articulate what really fires them up, makes them who they are or spurs them into action.

Shakespeare was right when he said, *"To thine own self be true."* When the day draws to a close, when your colleagues nstituents are not around, when the hustle and bustle has subsided, you have to be able to look yourself in the mirror and feel good about the person peering back at you. First and foremost, you are accountable to yourself. But how can you hold yourself accountable if you have not taken the time to reflect on who you are, why you choose to lead and what matters to you most? You can't. And you owe it to everyone around you to make a commitment to find out.

Defining purpose in work, life and business is not about the daily tasks, it's about the *reason* for the tasks in the first place — the *why*, not the *what*. Discovering purpose allows us to create the vision behind the tasks and knowing that vision can dramatically change results.

Knowing your purpose is the base of your personal foundation and defines your reason for living. While a leader can be busy with a million goals and tasks every day, when they do not have a clear purpose, they are at the mercy of others who will try to define their purpose for them. Without a sense of direction how is it possible to lead others? Where will you lead them?

The clearer you become about your purpose, the better you will be as a leader of others. I have yet to meet or read about an effective leader who did not have a strong underlying sense of purpose. Even if they were not yet doing the main thing they wanted in life, they had a sense of direction and conviction about who they were and why they were here, which gave them an edge.

What Is Purpose?

'What is my purpose?' is asked over and over at every stage of life. Chief executives, chairmen of boards, managers, community leaders and college students all rack their brains trying to determine their purpose as all sorts of philosophies are spread out before them like food at a restaurant buffet. Empty nesters restart the quest when their children have moved out. As their health and abilities decline, the elderly often wonder what purpose they still have.

There are many definitions of purpose. All agree it:

1. **Reveals** the deeper truth of who you are and the talents you naturally possess as an individual and as a leader.
2. **Aligns** all aspects of your life (career, romance, health, family, community, spirituality, finance).
3. **Guides** you: it is a compass for your life, a decision-making tool that empowers you to set firm boundaries and make purpose-aligned choices.

Purpose is deeply personal. It is about finding your place in the larger scheme of things, thoroughly loving what you do, being so energised by your calling that you feel compelled to shout at the top of your lungs, "This is what I was meant to do!"

Discovering Your Purpose As A Leader

Purpose is an individual thing and can take a long time to discover. Finding it isn't easy. If it were, we would all know exactly why we were here and we would be living that purpose every minute of every day. There can be a lot of trial and error and often a variety of pathways on the journey to self-discovery. However, there are some common themes, which most leaders will relate to. Purpose:

- Is built on the foundation of becoming confident in who you are and what gifts, passions and skills you have to contribute.
- Is related to passion. It can awaken inner passion that enables life-changing decisions and gives strength to endure testing situations.
- Is often related to being the best version of yourself that you can be, and helping others on that same journey.
- Is linked to leaving a legacy and making the world a better place. We all have a desire to make a mark. This is not necessarily about being famous or rich, but about making a difference.
- Involves tasks and may involve making money. But if it is only about those things, it will not necessarily lead to contentment or fulfilment. Purpose provides the big 'WHY' behind the drive to have money and perform tasks.

- Encourages you to follow your instinct instead of following the crowd.
- Motivates you on your journey even (or especially) when you encounter failure or rejection.
- Empowers your effective communication.

Consequences Of Not Finding Your Purpose

As an individual and a leader, there are consequences to not knowing or finding your purpose. There are men and women who have become successful in their work or relationships (their outer lives) and yet they feel hollow, empty, unfulfilled (their inner being). They describe feeling 'off-track' in some way, or incomplete, despite a conventionally successful life. Sometimes they wonder if they have been on the 'wrong' path all along — chosen the wrong career, or the wrong partner.

One thing is clear: there are consequences to not finding your purpose, including:

- chronic, lingering dissatisfaction; and
- an absence of inner peace and a sense of not being fully in sync with yourself. That is because your true inner self knows that your life purpose is out of sync with your outer life. The latter is often a false self, but you have identified with it because it's been so rewarding to your ego.

Point In Action

Fiona Moore★ is a leader of a very successful media company, which has offices across the globe. She is a household name and has a reputation of delivering exceptional services. She has played a key role in the expansion of her company and is the envy of most senior leaders.

Referred by a mutual colleague, Fiona met with me and I was inspired by her story of finding her purpose. She shared with me how four years ago (2012) she found herself in a place she had never been to before. Despite her skyrocketing business successes, she had lost her passion for what she was doing. Waking up was a chore and going to work required all the energy she had. She tried all sorts of things like meditation, decreasing her work hours and socialising with friends but still she felt a void. She knew something was missing but could not find what it was. The commotions inside her made her feel like an imposter because she continued giving talks on how to be successful when she knew that internally, she was not successful. This dissonance almost drove her to breaking broke.

One day, as she browsed the internet, Fiona came across Simon Sinek's book, *Start with why: How great leaders inspire others to take action* (2011). She was fascinated and started reading it. In the book Sinek says, "People don't buy WHAT you do, they buy WHY you do it." Finding your 'why' before communicating your 'what' or 'how' is critical to both business success and personal growth. If you do not know your purpose, you cannot clearly communicate or effectively execute your mission.

The statements in the book struck a chord with Fiona, who began her journey to find what her real purpose was. She enlisted the support of an executive coach. She realised that much of her life so far had been driven by other people's definitions of success and value systems rather than her own. Her lack of clarity on her personal purpose challenged her. She began looking at her purpose by exploring her values and beliefs. People who lead with purpose are clear about their values and beliefs. They stand by them and make supporting decisions. Others do not easily influence them, because they know what's most important. As a result, other people clearly know what they are about and view them as having high integrity.

This clarity of purpose (values, beliefs and passion) helped Fiona rethink her career and life choices. By identifying her CORE and her WHY, she began a process of aligning them with her life choices. She was amazed at how she was able to restore her passion for life by paying attention and following her purpose. It proved to her that she had the right to feel fulfilled by her work and that she did not have to suffer through her job or career.

This revelation was so powerful to Fiona that now she devotes her time trying to help others achieve the same thing. She did not quit her job but she was able to do it with clarity of purpose, in alignment with her value system. She introduced an internal mentoring programme for other leaders in her organisations, where she now helps others to identify their purpose.

*Not her real name

Characteristics of Leaders Who Find Their Purpose

Those who find their true purpose for being have some things in common:

1. **They are not preoccupied with self-interest.** That can sound contradictory. How can you find your life purpose if you are not focused on yourself? The fact is, when you are focused on yourself, with getting your goals or needs met (whether in work or relationships), your purpose becomes obscured. Your ego covers it, like clouds blocking the sun. Self-interest, or ego in this sense, is part of being human, of course. It is something that requires effort and consciousness to move through and let it go.

   Letting go of self-interest opens the door to recognising your true self more clearly, so you can see whether it is joined with your outer life, either creating a sense of purpose or clashing with it. Knowing who you are inside (your true values, secret desires, imagination; your capacity for love, empathy and generosity) all relate to and inform your life purpose.

2. **They use their mental and creative energy to serve something larger than themselves**. That is, they are like the lover who simply gives love for its own sake, without wanting something in return, without asking to be loved back or viewing their actions as a transaction or investment. That can be hard to imagine in our mercantile society, but giving your mental, emotional and creative energy from the heart comes naturally when you serve something larger than your self-interest.

Serving something beyond ego is always visible in those who have found their purpose, no matter their age. Sometimes it's by conscious intent. For example, letting go of a previous path when they awaken to it not being in sync with their inner self. Sometimes it's triggered by unanticipated events that answer an inner yearning.

Addressing Self-Interest Issues

As a leader, if you work towards weakening the stranglehold of self-interest, you can take an important step towards discovering your life's purpose: learning from your choices and way of life. That is, they can give you important feedback about the path you have been on, in relation to your deeper life purpose.

1. **Begin by examining your choices, way of life and commitments, looking from 'outside' yourself.** Try to discern what the outcomes (successes or failures) reveal about your inner self. Look for where there seems to be resonance or where it's missing. That is, don't try to 'find' your purpose by tweaking or fine-tuning what you have been doing in your work, relationships or anything else. Instead, let all of that teach you what it can. Look at what it tells you about your longings, your inner vision and predilections that you might be trying to express through your outer life, even if the latter may be the incorrect vehicle.

2. **When you do feel a pull towards some purpose, activity or goal that you feel reflects your inner self, pursue it fully and vigorously, with great intent.** Keep looking for the feedback your actions give you along the way. It does not matter if your purpose is concrete or spiritual. If you pursue it with minimal self-interest, with 'obliquity', you will learn from what happens if it is the true path for you or not.

3. **Infuse all your actions with a spirit of giving, of service; in effect, with love for what you are engaging with.** That includes all the people you interact with. The more you consciously infuse your thoughts, emotions and behaviour with positive, life-affirming energy — kindness, compassion, generosity, justice — the more you are keeping your ego at bay and can see your true purpose with greater

clarity. Of course, this is hard and you might encounter opposition from cultural pressures or others who have their own interests at stake. Keep in mind something Ralph Waldo Emerson wrote, "Whatever course you decide upon, there is always someone to tell you that you are wrong. There are always difficulties arising that tempt you to believe that your critics are right. To map out a course of action and follow it to an end requires courage."

Reflective Questions

1. What drives you? When you are relaxing with friends, what do you love talking about? Is there a theme that makes you feel animated?
2. What interest or passion are you most afraid of admitting?
3. When you were a child, what did you want to be when you grew up? What childhood dreams did you have?
4. Fear of failure stunts our dreams and actions. What would you do if you knew you would not fail?
5. What would you do if money was no barrier?
6. What would be the smallest step towards your following your passion?

Chapter 3: Receiving Feedback

"The road to self-insight runs through other people."
David Dunning

"If you are irritated by every rub how will you be polished."
Rumi

As a leader, receiving feedback is one of the critical ways that helps you see yourself as others see you. Conversely, it is also through feedback that others know how you see them.

The previous chapter highlighted how receiving feedback is one of the best ways to increase self-awareness. Feedback is any

> *It is your responsibility to become the best version of yourself*

kind of return information or instruction that is helpful in regulating behaviour, and can have any source. It takes the form of verbal or nonverbal communication, and gives you information about how your behaviour is perceived by one or more individuals, particularly performance appearance. Others define feedback as a reaction to how your behaviour affects other people, usually in terms of their emotions and perceptions.

People usually say they want constructive feedback, but not everyone is equipped to receive it openly and in a way that makes it worthwhile. Therefore, it is important as a leader to get continuous feedback on your impact.

Imagine waking up after a good night's sleep and discovering some of your feedback systems are not working. You can see and hear, but you cannot recognise anything in the room. You are conscious, and you know you should be in your bedroom, but nothing seems familiar. You're also aware that you can't feel the sheets against your body. You want to walk, but without feeling in your legs, you simply crumble to the floor. Even if you can walk, you have no idea where you're going.

Can you imagine the fear that might overwhelm you? We're so accustomed to receiving and understanding essential information from our environment that we take feedback for granted. I think you will agree that a simple act of getting out of bed to make a cup of coffee is both a gift and a blessing.

Feedback systems in our bodies protect us. Positive feedback tells us to eat when we're hungry and stop when we're full. Negative feedback is similarly important. Just imagine not feeling pain when you touch something hot — you could experience severe physical damage without knowing it.

People react differently to feedback. Some:

- **Openly deny it**. Doing so sends the message of not being open to feedback, which is the exact opposite of the message you want to send. You will have a strong temptation to deny unflattering feedback, even though it may be true. Also, the more intense your emotional reaction is when denying feedback, the more you validate the content to others. You are going to want to remain emotionally calm, even in denial.
- **Listen, but not act**. This also sends a dangerous message. People will end up not bothering.
- **Listen, understand and use it**. This shows you understand the critical role feedback plays in helping you to get where you want and achieve what you want. This is something I learnt the hard way.

Point in action

Five years ago, I was an executive coach for Michael*, Director of Estates in a large communications organisation. As part of his development, he agreed to undertake a 360-degree feedback assessment. He was very confident in his talent as a leader and told me he was committed to improving his skills. I sent a link to Michael's colleagues, customers, subordinates, manager and others to ask for their thoughts, and the feedback turned out not to be what Michael expected. In fact, he did not like the results.

Michael assessed his leadership skills quite differently to the survey respondents. While he saw himself as open to other people's ideas, the respondents said he was autocratic and controlling. What Michael saw as honesty and commitment to the growth of his staff and the organisation, came across to the feedback providers as arrogance and a tendency to be overly critical.

This assessment gave Michael a significant growth opportunity, but, like many people who dislike feedback responses, Michael discounted the survey results. He told himself that the respondents misunderstood the instrument, that they saw him inaccurately and that the results did not reflect his true leadership persona. He blocked an opportunity for growth by rationalising away the unexpectedly negative feedback.

Fortunately, Michael spent some time thinking objectively about the information the survey produced. He worked through his initial response, moved beyond his bias and carefully evaluated the feedback. He learnt to acknowledge it as constructive criticism even though he did not like it, and to recognise the growth opportunity it presented.

As Michael opened himself up to hearing what others had to say about his job performance, he found ways to behave differently. Most importantly, his new-found understanding of his own reaction to the feedback process showed him how he had reacted similarly when people presented ideas that did not fit his way of doing things. Michael realised his behaviour had created an environment that not only discouraged the honesty he claimed to want, but actually punished people whose methods clashed with his own. Honest feedback provides leaders with valuable opportunities to grow.

*not his real name

Remember that not all feedback is necessarily valid. However, it is important for our own continuous development to know what we evoke or provoke in other people.

How To Ask For Feedback

In order to effectively ask for feedback, think about:

1. **Who you ask.** Start with an employee or individual you trust and know well, and ask them for feedback on something small.
2. **How you ask.** Don't ask vague questions like, 'What do you think?' Ask specifics about the topic at hand.
3. **When you ask.** Allow for a chance to give a thoughtful answer. That means, ask the question(s) ahead of time.

4. **Where you ask.** You might receive more honest feedback in an informal setting, rather than at your desk in the office.

5. **How you respond.** If you really want feedback, you have to be prepared to shut up and listen. Qualifying or clarifying questions is okay, but be mindful not to act offended.

How To Receive Feedback

If you hear something and immediately disagree, don't voice it. It makes the situation uncomfortable and creates a defence-attack scenario that is notoriously challenging. Feedback also changes over time. In the bigger picture, what may be true today may no longer be true tomorrow. What you are hearing is one angle and not all feedback is useful. Just as much as we cannot possibly know every part of our own self with complete accuracy, neither can another person. What may be true in one set of circumstances may not be true in another. What one person observes might be different from what someone else sees.

Reflection Questions

1. How receptive are you to feedback?
2. What is the relationship between you wanting honest feedback and the way you react after receiving it?
3. What is your reaction to honest feedback? Do you become defensive when you hear it?

4. Are you eager to hear honest feedback? Do you tell the people around you?

5. What changes will make it easier for you to hear feedback?

Chapter 4:
Acknowledge Your Blind Spots

Any single peron's viewpoint will have blind spots
caused by their habitual ways of perceiving the world,
their perception filters.... How can we shift our
perceptions to get outside our own limited world view?
John Seymours

"As a leader, 1st, work on yourself- increase your self-
awareness. There shouldn't be any other urgent agenda
than this. Get enlightened! Know very well who you're
including your strengths, weaknesses, and blind spots!"
Assegid Habtewold

What Are Blind Spots?

Recently, I had a near-miss as I drove away from a parking bay; I had not seen that another car was coming. This is called a blind spot. The larger your blind spots are, the more dangerous they become. As a leader, you have blind spots no matter how brilliant and accomplished you are. There will be parts of your behaviour that you may not understand and you may not realise the impact it has on others and yourself.

To be a successful leader who is self-aware, you need to become intimate with your strengths and your blind spots, those aspects of your personality that can derail you. John C. Maxwell defines a blind spot as "an area in the lives of people in which they continually do not see themselves or their situation realistically". Blind spots, the skills that leaders overestimate, are more problematic. These are weaknesses leaders can't see in themselves even though they are evident to everyone around them.

> *Overplaying strengths is often rooted in some deeper insecurity that must be acknowledged to dial back the overcompensation*

In her book, *Fearless leadership* (2009), leadership expert Loretta Malandro highlights that "blind spots can be overplayed strengths". She goes on to say that "Doing too much of something can be a problem as doing too little of it. Those strengths that got you where you are can become our derailers if not adapted as needed to new leadership roles. Overplaying strengths is often rooted in some deeper insecurity that must be acknowledged to be able to dial back the overcompensation. For example, being forceful turns into being dogmatic; consensus seeking breeds chronic indecision; being respectful of others degenerates into ineffectual niceness; and the desire to turn a profit and serve shareholders becomes a preoccupation with short-term thinking." She goes on to say, "in good times blind spots are annoying and frustrating; in tough times they can be lethal".

Projection

The challenges in dealing with our blind spots can stem from within. Our blind spots can sometimes turn into 'allergies': behaviours we don't like and project onto other people. A projection is a trait, attitude, feeling or behaviour that actually belongs to your own personality, but is not experienced as such. Instead, you attribute it to objects or people in your environment, then experience it as directed toward you by them, instead of the other way round.

In other words, to project is to place what we do not want to acknowledge ownership of outside of ourselves. Usually this is something we don't like about ourselves. Often we can associate what we don't like in others with what we don't like in ourselves. In his book, *Facilitation* (2000), Trevor Bentley describes that: "In order for our clients to understand their own projections we work through a four-stage exercise:

1. Identify what you don't like in yourself.
2. Share this with someone else using the statement, 'What I do not like about myself is…'

3. Now imagine seeing this in someone else and notice what you feel and how you react.

4. Imagine again seeing what you don't like about yourself in someone else and this time imagine that you feel and react differently. In other words, break your own pattern. The way through this impasse is to take ownership by working on our projections."

This exercise is really useful when working with others to identify their blind spots and projections.

The Johari Window

The Johari Window is one of the many ways of assessing your blind spots and the awareness that others have about you. The model was devised by American psychologists Joseph Luft and Harry Ingham in 1955.

Open pane/known self	Hidden pane/hidden self
The things you know about yourself and reveal to others; your public personality.	The things you keep to yourself.
Includes, for instance, your gender, height and messages you intentionally disclose to people.	This might include your favourite drink, your default personality preferences. You can reduce your hidden pane by sharing these parts of yourself with others

	(disclosure) because if you hide too much, you could come across as secretive and people may not trust you.
Blind self The things people know about you that you are unaware of. This is where friends' honesty can come in handy.	**Unknown self** The things neither you nor others know about you that can affect your relationships with others.

The most interesting pane is the 'blind self' — what others know about you that would benefit you to know. In our daily lives, we have a pretty good feel for what we 'know' and we manoeuvre our behaviour around it. Unfortunately, the insights from our blind spots are not routinely on our radar screens. We only get those insights if we seek them out or pay attention when they come our way unsolicited. Seeking feedback about your blind spots will reduce them and increase the open free area.

We could be much more effective in our leadership if we were able to harvest — and act on — the feedback from these blind spots. The real challenge is that people skills become much more pronounced as one goes higher up the chain of command, hence the real need for senior leaders in particular to grasp this concept.

Why Pay Attention To Blind Spots?

Blind spots are perhaps the single best predictor of low ratings in performance appraisal (Lombardo and Eichinger, 2009). They can result in destructive behaviour, such as defensiveness, lack of humility, insensitivity, and a tendency to be over-controlling or overly assertive.

Leaders often succeed by being aware of their blind spots. One blind spot can undermine your strong leadership abilities. They are called blind spots because we are unaware of them. The fact is, knowing yourself isn't as easy as it sounds. Leaders have the power to shield themselves from painful and difficult truths and followers may collude with this. As a result, leaders are often more prone to blind spots.

As a leader progresses or roles change, blind spots that used to be tolerated can become highly problematic. When those blind spots are not recognised and addressed in a timely manner, leaders find themselves in trouble.

Common Blind Spots

- **Overestimating strategic capability**. This is often the blind spot of leaders with strong operational backgrounds, who are promoted into higher levels of an organisation where their role is more strategic. Rather than seek help, they address strategic challenges as operational challenges. The default way of dealing with challenges is seeing everything as a problem to be solved when sometimes it's a dilemma to be managed. Some leaders from operational backgrounds are driven to deliver on their priorities and, as a result, can miss 'weak signals', or important facts that are easy to overlook. This is particularly true when leaders are operating under tight deadlines.

> *One blind spot can undermine your strong leadership abilities*

- **Valuing being right over being effective**. This blind spot occurs when a leader thinks they already know the answer or best course of action, so is unwilling to listen to others. They may even interrupt people, or call conversations to a conclusion. Their followers quickly learn it's a waste of time to raise contrary opinions and ideas. I had a manager like this at one point in my career and I decided just to go with the flow. Unfortunately, that particular organisation did not get the best out of me.

- **Failing to balance the 'what' with the 'how'.** This blind spot occurs when leaders focus on an organisation's measurable results. In extreme situations, this can lead their followers to short-term thinking, or worse, unethical behaviours.

- **Not seeing your impact on others**. This occurs when you assume all of your followers have the same motivations, communication style, goals and values as you. This leads to confusion and frustration while working as a team. Again, this is where projection usually comes in.
- **Thinking the present is the past**. Often personal flaws are shrugged off and new challenges ignored because what has worked in the past led to the present-day success. These leaders don't recognise that what got them to one place may not get them where they want to go next.

Point In Action

A few years ago I got a phone call from Sarah★, a client I was coaching. She sounded very distressed and requested that we have our coaching session four weeks before the scheduled date. I asked her what was going on and all she said was that she was fed up with people wanting her to be someone else. I agreed to meet with her earlier.

When we met, Sarah told me that during a meeting, one member of her team had highlighted how she sometimes came across as abrupt, unsupportive and selfish. This was news to Sarah and her immediate reaction was, why has no one ever mentioned it to me before? She looked around the room hoping that other members of her direct reports would support her and say this man was mad. Unfortunately, there were nods in agreement. Sarah was heartbroken and felt that people were ganging up against her. She saw it as upward bullying and was not very happy.

From a young age, Sarah had been a high achiever, getting a number of accolades along the way. Her lowest results were always outstanding. Because she was so driven, she quickly rose to the position of Managing Director in a very successful organisation.

Sarah was just unable to shake this feedback. It occupied her thoughts and she started planning devious ways of ousting her 'haters'. However, a part of her also wondered if the feedback was true. This possibility rocked her to the core. For the first time, she was facing a side of her she never knew existed.

Fast forward to our meeting. What she had experienced was opening herself up to the 'blind spot', shown in the Johari Window.

*not her real name

Addressing Your Blind Spots

It's one thing to know what your blind spots are but without doing something about them, it's meaningless. The following six practices offer some daily disciplines to help you learn and overcome potential blind spots:

1. **Raise your awareness of your blind spots.** We all have blind spots. What differs is our level of

awareness. Leaders are often surprised when people complain about their blind spots or perceived blind spots. Knowing and identifying your blind spots means you are one step closer to becoming an effective leader. You can't address what you don't know.

2. **Consider the downside of your strengths.** It's a known fact that our gifts taken to the extreme can be liabilities. List all your strengths and reflect on how they manifest themselves in your leadership style. If you need help, work with a mentor or coach. Consider asking your colleagues for feedback.

3. **Examine your history.** To gain insight into behaviour that may not serve you well, think back on your past successes and failures as a leader. This kind of introspective inventory can yield some powerful insights. What do you need to stop doing because it has not served you well? What do you need to do more of? What do you need to start doing? What patterns are there in both verbal and non-verbal feedback from those around you?

4. **Understand your habits.** Blind spots are not necessarily weaknesses; they can also be habits or instinctive reactions to situations. For example, does your workload cause you to interrupt people in meetings to speed up things? If it does, work on developing more patience. It will enhance your interpersonal skills and improve your leadership.

5. **Establish a peer-coaching arrangement.** Every leader can benefit from peer coaching with people

they trust. This is refered to as action learning provides a powerful way to encourage self-managed, active learning.

6. **Overcome defensiveness.** Know what makes you defensive; learn to recognise your defensive behaviour and put strategies in place to overcome it.

If you learn to master your blind spots, you start to accelerate your learning.

Reflection Questions

1. What are your blind spots?
2. How accurately do you assess your job performance or relationships with different individuals?
3. What feedback would you like, to understand where you can develop?
4. How often are you surprised by feedback on your performance?
5. Who else do you need to get an honest perspective on your blind spots?

Chapter 5: Growth Edges

"Life begins at the end of your comfort zone."
Neale Donald Walsch

"Be willing to step outside your comfort zone once in a while; take the risks in life that seem worth taking."
Edward Whitacre Jr.

Growth Edges

Our growth edges start where we become aware of our blind spots; it is where learning starts. It is also the point at which good and great leaders separate. If you are serious about your development as a leader, the journey is continuous with no destination. Personal growth requires pushing against the very edge of your comfort zone; it can be an uncertain and scary place. It's a big ask to always be at your best in a leadership role. The growth edge is a challenge that makes you feel excited and want to move ahead while also feeling scared and hesitant. Another definition from the Street Dictionary is "our growing edge is that area of your life where there's still a lot of room for improvement but you're pushing ahead and stretching the margins of that area every day.

If something is alive it is always growing. There is always the next shoot, bud or growing edge. A tree is a good example, if you look at the shoots on a branch that are just coming into existence. This is where the tree is most vital. It is where the trees life force is the strongest. It is where there is the greatest degree of aliveness.

These growing edges have several distinct properties:

- They are fragile and vulnerable, without any bark protecting them against the elements.
- They are soft and have the green colour of new life.
- They are unique to that branch of the tree. While all trees share the same process of growth, each branch looks different depending on the unique circumstances and stage of its growth.
- There is no right growing edge for a tree. There certainly is no way to say, one growing edge is better than another or one branch should be like another branch.

If there are no new growing edges coming into existence than the tree is atrophying and moving toward death."

Growth edges give strength and stability as 'roots'. There are areas that continue to change and grow very slowly. This might be the bark on a tree. For some people, taste in clothes, music, certain food and similar things grow through the years, but remain fairly steady overall. Then there are the vulnerable edges, where newness extends outward, the new branches and new leaves of your life. New jobs, relationships, learning, turns on the spiritual path, areas of growth, areas of vitality, areas of uniqueness.

Sheryl Sandberg in her book *Lean in: Women, work and the will to lead (2013),* highlights that "Paying attention to your growth edge exposes you to formerly hidden aspects of your leadership". Some leaders are scared away by how much they need to grow. Great leaders will enjoy the process and start intentionally working on their growth areas. According to author and motivational speaker, Les Brown, "if you put yourself in a position where you have to stretch outside your comfort zone, then you are expanding your consciousness". Working on your growth edges helps you understand the limitations of your current ways of thinking so that you can expand those limitations if you choose.

Point in action
Extract from unknown source

"It is like if you catch hold of a fish in the sea and you throw it on the shore; the fish jumps back into the sea. Now for the first time it will know that it has always lived in the sea; for the first time it will know that, "the sea is my life". Up to now, before it was caught and thrown on the shore, it may not ever have thought of the sea at all; it may have been utterly oblivious of the sea. To know something, first you have to lose it. To be aware of paradise, first you have to lose it. Unless it is lost *and* regained you will not understand the beauty of it."

Working On Your Growth Edges

Facing growth edges is transformational. It doesn't just change what you know, it changes the way you know, enabling new capabilities for managing complexity, stress and change. By having an insight into the characteristic ways we make sense of our worlds, we become more aware, take more control and have more choices and a bigger perspective on our lives and organisations.

Our view of the world influences every aspect of our lives. It affects the sense we make of our organisations, our work, our relationships and ourselves.

Reflection Questions

1. What is your growth edge? How do you know?
2. To what extent are you being intentional about your learning and growth edge? What else can you do about this?
3. Do you always perform the way you want to or are capable of? If not, why?

4. How do you make decisions when you are at your 'edge moments'?
5. What were your decisions in those moments?

Chapter 6:
Personality Preferences

"Always be yourself, have faith in yourself, do not go out and look for a successful personality and duplicate it." **Bruce Lee**

"Cute is when a personality shines through their looks." **Natalie Portman**

What Is Personality?

Personality is something we informally assess and describe every day. When we talk about ourselves and others, we frequently refer to different characteristics of each individual's personality. Therefore, understanding your own personality is one of the key factors of successful leadership. A leader is most effective when their strongest personality traits are engaged.

We all have our own preferences, that is, what you like and operate within. These preferences typically allow us to be efficient, effective and our most-comfortable selves. Conversely, operating outside these limits requires more time and energy and usually results in lower-quality work. Understanding these limits — and knowing when you're inside or outside them — can improve your productivity, efficiency and time-management skills.

Personality type matters because it affects everything we think, say and do. It impacts group dynamics and how we relate to other people. It is at the heart of good and bad relationships. It is partially responsible for how we act in conflict, under stress and during times of change. It impacts how we innovate, mentor, lead, manage and problem solve. It influences time-management behaviour, attentiveness in meetings, goal-setting approaches and motivation.

Leadership and Personality Development

As a leader in any context, you will commonly encounter a mix of different personalities, viewpoints, experiences, expectations, communication issues and conflicts. A number of questions arise:

- How can you get such different people to work as an effective team?
- How do you improve communication? How can you resolve and prevent conflict?
- How can you help others succeed in today's fast-paced environment?

- How do you establish an effective work environment? How do you increase workplace productivity and job satisfaction?
- How do you motivate employees and become a better leader?

Benefits of Knowing Your Personality Preferences

1. When you understand yourself, you can improve quickly and more easily by addressing the right thoughts and behaviour. Knowing your personality type gives you the insights you need to develop a personal growth plan.
2. You learn that people aren't wrong, they're different, and different is good.
3. You can be reassured that you're not crazy. Knowing your personality type isn't an excuse, but it is an incredible tool for understanding why some situations are tough and it will help you get through them.
4. You can better manage your day-to-day routines. When you understand what you need to thrive, you can structure your day accordingly.
5. You can recognise why you feel out of sorts, and know how to deal with it.
6. You can learn to manage your energy.

Tools for Developing Leadership Capability

When used well, personality tools can offer remarkable insights that help you develop high levels of self-awareness and improve the way you interact with others and the world around you.

There are many instruments that assess self-awareness, various styles and deal with differences among personality traits. They offer you the potential to choose how you want to be and how to change — in this case, developing your capability as a leader. There are far too many personality tools to discuss here, so I have selected two that I find useful.

1. **Myers Briggs Type Indicator (MBTI)** is one of the most frequently used tools in leadership development programmes around the world. It provides information about a person's preferred style of behaving and thinking and can help build self-awareness and emotional intelligence. MBTI assessment can be accessed on www.opp.com.

2. **FIRO-B** is an accessible and universally applicable framework that reveals how individuals can shape and adapt their behaviour, influence others effectively and build trust among colleagues. It is an excellent resource for coaching individuals and teams about the underlying drivers behind their interactions with others www.opp.com.

Personality tools are a useful starting point for discussions on heightening your self-awareness. However, it is important to have a specialist help you interpret the results from any personality test.

Point in action

Council X had issues to do with leadership development. Over a three-year period, there was an unhealthy turnover of staff and exit interview data highlighted leadership unhealthy behaviour as one of the pain points. The Chief Executive had tried all forms of interventions, from restructuring to sending people on courses and transformation programmes. However, change was not happening at the right pace.

Following extensive conversations with staff and other key stakeholders, the Chief Executive decided to bring in consultants to help him develop and deliver a leadership development programme.

After the initial conversations, the consultants recognised that the main challenge for the council's leadership was to do with personality clashes, which resulted in behavioural difficulties. This required a cultural change. The consultants suggested the use of MBTI personality assessment tools for the different levels of leaders.

The Chief Executive was very clear on wanting to avoid the idea of 'more and less' or 'better and worse'. The MBTI personality tool provided that for them as it genuinely appreciated the differences in people, and worked with that difference in a positive and constructive way to get the best out of everyone. Three months after the end of the programme, this is what participants were saying:

"I now understand why X always respond this way"

"I now appreciate that I am not always the crazy one"

"I have an idea on what I need to do to be able to make an impact"

"I can now see that my reality is not the only reality, there are multiple realities"

Reflection Questions

1. To what extent are you aware of your personality preferences? What are they? How can you become more aware of them?
2. What aspects of your personality preferences serve you well? What aspects do you need to work on?
3. How do you relate to others? Are you comfortable working with people with different preferences and styles to yours?
4. How do you assign work? What do you expect from the work of others? How do you complete work yourself?
5. How do your personality preferences (expressiveness, assertiveness and flexibility) affect your personal energy levels? Do you gain or lose energy around other people?

Chapter 7: Leadership style

"Ignorance is the key to avoidance,
but arrogance promotes avoidance."
Norbert Hams

"For those of you who really want to give critical
thought to your unique leadership style and foster
genuine followership, learn from what's out there
and weave it into something meaningful and authentic."
Stacy Feiner

Why Pay Attention To Your Leadership Style?

Your leadership style encompasses how you relate to others inside and outside your immediate area or organisation, how you view yourself and your position and, to a large extent, whether you are successful as a leader. According to Newstrom and Davis, leadership experts and authors of *Leadership management: principles, models and theories 1993,* "leadership style is the manner and approach of providing direction, implementing plans, and motivating people". It includes the total pattern of explicit and implicit actions you perform as a leader.

Your leadership style has a significant effect on the culture of the organisation you work for and the people you work with. In many ways, your style as a leader defines your organisation. If your organisation is faithful to its mandate, your leadership style must be consistent with that. For example, an autocratic leader in a democratic organisation can create chaos. A leader concerned only with the bottom line in an organisation built on the importance of human values may undermine the purpose of its work.

The leadership style you choose (yes, to a great extent, it is an active choice) has a direct impact on the result you achieve. It is what makes you memorable to others and fulfilled within yourself.

Types Of Leadership Style

There are many types of leadership style. Different styles fit different situations and a leader will need to decide which fits their particular situation. Consciously or subconsciously, you will no doubt use some of the leadership styles listed below, at least some of the time. By understanding these leadership styles and their impact, you can become a more flexible, better leader.

If you're leading well, you won't have just one leadership style. You will mix and match to engage your team and meet your goals. No one style of leadership fits all situations, so it's useful to understand different leadership frameworks and styles. You can then adapt your approach to fit your situation.

Leadership Styles

Leader-ship style	Characteristics	Impact on others
Charismatic	■	• Can create risk that a project or group will flounder if leader leaves • Leader's feeling of invincibility can ruin a team by taking on too much risk • Team success seen as directly connected to the leader's presence
Bureaucratic/command control	• Follows rules rigorously and ensures people follow procedures precisely **This leadership type suits situations:** • Involving serious safety risks (such as working with machinery, with toxic substances, or at dangerous heights), or	• If used too much, it can feel restrictive and limits others' ability to develop their own leadership skills • Others have little chance to debrief what was learned before next encounter with leader • Less effective in teams and organisations that rely on flexibility, creativity, or innovation

	with large sums of money • Involving managing employees who perform routine tasks • Demanding immediate compliance	
Laissez faire	• Gives all the rights and power to make decisions to the worker • Knows what is happening but is not directly involved in it • Trusts others to keep their word • Monitors performance, gives feedback regularly **This leadership type suits situations when:** • The team is working in multiple locations or remotely • A project, under multiple leaders, must come together by a specific date • Quick results are needed from a highly cohesive team • Followers are highly skilled, experienced, and educated	• Followers could feel insecure at the unavailability of a leader • Effective when team is skilled, experienced, and self-directed in use of time and resources • Autonomy of team members leads to high job satisfaction and increased productivity

	• Followers have pride in their work and the drive to do it successfully on their own	
Servant leadership	• Lead simply by meeting the needs of the team, regardless of level • Puts service to others before self-interest • Includes the whole team in decision making • Provides tools to get the job done • Stays out of limelight, lets team accept credit for results **This leadership type suits situations:** • When leader is elected to a team, organisation, committee, or community • When anyone, at any level of the group, meets the needs of the team • Needing a leader with high integrity, who leads with generosity. • Their approach can create a positive	• Organisations with these leaders often seen on 'best places to work' lists • Can create a positive culture and lead to high morale • Ill suited if situation calls for quick decisions or meeting tight deadlines

	corporate culture, and can lead to high morale among team members	
Transformational	• Expects team to transform even when it's uncomfortable • Counts on everyone giving their best • Serves as a role model for all involved **This leadership type suits situations to:** • Encourage the group to pursue innovative and creative ideas and actions • Motivate the group by strengthening team optimism, enthusiasm, and commitment	• Can lead to high productivity and engagement from all team members • Team needs detailed-oriented people to ensure scheduled work is done

Choosing And Developing A Leadership Style

Many leaders are concerned about which style(s) to adopt. As highlighted above, it is important to realise that different styles may be appropriate at different times, and for different purposes. Almost all leaders, even great ones, have to learn how to lead and have to develop their skills. You can do the same, especially if you have a clear idea of what you think leadership is about, and if you have good models from which to learn.

Here are a few things you can do to choose and develop your own effective leadership style:

1. **Start with yourself**

   Knowing who you are is the first step toward both choosing a style and understanding what you'll have to do to adopt it. Be clear with yourself about what your natural tendencies and talents are. If you want to be a collaborative leader but tend to tell people what to do, you have to admit that and think about ways to change it. If you want to be a directive leader but you have trouble making decisions, you need to deal with that issue.

2. **Ask yourself what your organisation needs**

   You can adapt most styles to most situations, but don't neglect the real needs of the organisation in your calculations. You may need to practise a different style at the beginning from the one that you want to assume over the long term to solve problems in the organisation, or to get people on board.

3. **Learn from others**

   Think about how leaders you've worked for or with exercised their leadership. What were their styles and were they effective? How did they handle different situations? How did their actions make you and others feel? Try to watch others in action, and talk to them about how they see what they do. What do you like about how they operate? What don't you like? What can you incorporate into your own style?

4. **Be prepared to change**

Although this may seem at odds with some of the above, it is probably the most important element to good leadership. No matter how well you're doing, it's not perfect — it never is, and never will be. Be prepared to find or hear the negative as well as the positive, consider it carefully and objectively, and make corrections if necessary. That way, you will not only become a good leader, but continue to be one.

Reflection Questions

1. How great is your need to be in control?
2. How willing are you to trust others to do their jobs? Are you uncomfortable delegating work, and just try to do it yourself? Do you tell people exactly how to do things, even when they have experience?
3. How patient are you? Do you interrupt with your comments before others are finished speaking? Do you want the discussion to end because you want to start *doing* something?
4. How organised are you? Can you find what you need without having to search for it? Is your desk clean?
5. How good are your people skills? When you're with others, do you spend most of your time talking? Listening? Do people seek you out for help or advice?

Chapter 8:
Authentic Leadership

"The task of leadership is not to put greatness into humanity, but to elicit it, for greatness is already there".
John Buchan

"Truth is a point of view, but authenticity can't be faked."
Peter Guber

In today's world, there is a chorus of calls from global news articles and various lobby groups for more authentic leadership. These calls abound because of the growing cynicism that many people have expressed regarding leaders around the globe who seem to pad their own pockets at the expense of their people and the organisations they serve. We live in an era in which authentic leaders who share values with their people — shareholders, stakeholders, employees, customers or constituents — are the ones who have a true and lasting impact.

The idea of authentic leadership has been around for a long time, although it had different names until Bill George's book, *Authentic leadership*, popularised the term in 2003. Since then, it has become business jargon, often overused and not understood well enough to be meaningful. But there is something behind the jargon — ideas and concepts that have been around for centuries that can help leaders lead people by having a sense of self-awareness, identity, honesty and passion.

At its most basic level, authenticity means being genuine — not a replica, copy or imitation. In leadership, being genuine implies we are embodying our true selves in our leadership role. Being true to ourselves calls us to draw on the very essence of our values, beliefs, principles, morals and use this to create our 'guiding compass' in the job. Not somebody else's compass, our own! Authentic leadership means making the most of our strengths, recognising and trading off our weaknesses and taking full accountability for the impact we have on others. What authentic leadership is not about is adopting the styles or traits of other leaders.

Daniel Goleman and Bill George in their book, *The executive edge: an insider's guide to outstanding leadership* (2015), describes authentic leadership as a leadership style that is consistent with a leader's personality and core values, and is honest, ethical and practical. Authentic leadership creates a desire for connection; other people would naturally want to follow you. A true leader shows up authentically and is present. In this world of increasing demands, constant change and distractions, it is the authentic leader we crave.

Authentic leadership clearly depicts a higher level of moral reasoning and capacity to make judgments that goes beyond one's self-interest. Said another way, it includes one's self-interest to serve the collective interests of the group. Authentic leaders go through life continually revisiting their theory of the self that represents the beliefs, views, and evaluations they hold about themselves. This self-awareness and revision process allows them to determine how they can be better so that the collective can be better.

> *It is one thing to recognise an authentic leader, but another to become one*

Authenticity can be both owning your personal experiences (thoughts, emotions, or beliefs, the 'real me' inside), and acting in accord with your true self (behaving and expressing what you really think and believe). The authentic leader is confident, hopeful, optimistic, resilient, transparent, moral, ethical and future oriented.

You can learn from others, but there is no way you can be successful if you are trying to be like them. People seem to trust you when you are genuine and authentic, not a replica of someone else. For me, this is the start of authentic leadership. There is a lot of encouragement and pressure to bring our full selves to the workplace and to connect through personal stories as a way of earning trust and building effective connections.

You do not have to be born with specific characteristics or traits of a leader. Discovering your authentic leadership requires a commitment to developing yourself. Like musicians and athletes, you must devote yourself to a lifetime of realising your potential. Authentic leaders also keep a strong support team around them, ensuring that they live integrated and grounded lives.

The Key Behaviour Of An Authentic Leader

The central component of authentic leadership is being genuine, which means every authentic leader is different. However, there are several markers that these leaders tend to share.

Authentic Leaders:

- Demonstrate behaviours that enable you to trust them.
- Take ownership when they make mistakes and share responsibility for them.
- Show the necessary courage to push further up the leadership chain, to question the current status quo or defend their people and processes.
- Invite others' contributions and delegate meaningful work in the true spirit of recognising the inherent

abilities of others. Authentic leaders give responsibility to others and trust their innate capacity to perform the tasks not only as well as them, but perhaps even better.

- Practice values-based decision making and make their values known to their followers so they can judge their decisions.
- Act with integrity and stand for what they believe in. They are trustworthy and reliable.

There is a level of expectation around what a great leader should do and how they should behave. These expected norms can create myths about leaders being inspirational, exhibiting unrelenting confidence, having unwavering decision making, showing unshakeable self-belief and revealing no signs of personal weakness. In authentic leadership, while some of these may well help in the role, the real test is somewhat more grounded.

Point In Action

An example of an authentic leader who lives to transform others' lives for the better is Oprah Winfrey. Known all over the world by her first name, Oprah was born in rural Mississippi and raised by her grandmother until age six when she went to live with her mother. Oprah overcame many challenges, including being sexually abused when she was nine years old, to become one of the most dominant media personalities of modern America (Forbes.com). As a transformational leader, Oprah had a clear vision and mission best seen in her multi award-winning show, *The Oprah Winfrey Show*, where she influenced and inspired millions worldwide to dream big. *Time* magazine named her one of the most influential people of 2004, 2005, 2006, 2007, 2008 and 2009.

Oprah is known for basing her decisions and judgments on the premise of how others would be affected. She exhibits the qualities and competencies that the best business books, graduate schools and executive education programmes steer us to attain. One of Oprah's most-famous quotes is, "I had no idea that being your authentic self could make me as rich as I've become. If I had, I'd have done it a lot earlier."

Oprah's communication skills have enabled her to engage with people from diverse backgrounds. People have been able to identify with her because of her background and because she succeeded in a male-dominated world. She is known to shed a tear over emotional stories in her interviews; this human side of her connects her with people who see her as caring.

She is an authentic communicator who makes a strong connection with her audience. She also has a great sense of moral values. When Oprah makes mistakes, she is willing to announce that she was wrong. This is why so many of her viewers felt a strong connection with her.

Reflection Questions

1. How authentic is your leadership? How do you know?
2. What has helped you develop a sense of authenticity as a leader?
3. How do you think people experience you? How do you know?
4. What do you feel about how you come across?

Chapter 9:
Why Character Matters

*"The course of any society is largely
determined by the quality of its moral leadership."*
Anne Colby and William Damon

*"A person's true character is revealed
by what he does when no one else is watching."*
Unknown

T here are dozens of books on leadership, its styles
and development but leadership character is rarely
discussed. When we talk about character, we do not
mean personality. Your character is at the heart of who
you are as a leader and as an individual. It demonstrates
your moral and ethical compass to the outside world.
Unlike other qualities, character is not something you
are born with. No matter what your background is or
family circumstances are, you can make a conscious
decision about the type of person you want to be and

your character develops over time. People who lead from within are usually concerned about their character.

You will also find many organisations discussing leadership competencies but very few addressing leadership character. Leadership competencies determine what a person can do; character determines what they will do. Leadership is certainly about character, but that character needs to be enhanced by competence to be effective. On the other hand, competence and talent without character will not take you very far as a leader. As a leader in this rapidly changing world, you will need to continuously take stock of your character and its impact on others.

Character becomes more important as you move towards higher levels of leadership, because people need a leader who is clearly grounded in what they stand for, especially in times of change. With so many factors disrupting the work environment today, leaders with a well-developed sense of who they are can provide stability — the consistency of purpose and values that employees need to remain focused and on task, regardless of the level in the organization.

Most leadership development programmes focus on the 'form' — skills, tasks and behaviours. We also need to challenge leaders to reflect and think critically about their character, values and beliefs about themselves and their organisations.

The Importance Of Character

Your character as a leader shapes the culture of the environment you are in (whether society, church, organisation etc.). Your character is what others consistently experience when they are around you. Your conduct largely determines the influence you have over your 'followers'. In other words, who you really are influences how effective you will be in leading others. Ghandi, for example, believed his personal life gave him the credibility that enabled him to be a successful leader. If you want to be a great leader of others, you must first become a great leader of yourself.

Leaders without character often:

- hurt themselves by losing the trust of their colleagues and damaging their reputations;
- squander the confidence of their constituents and lose the respect of their peers; and
- forfeit once-loyal customers and watch their most-valued employees head for the door.

Most importantly, every time a leader displays weak character, they let themselves down. You must answer to your conscience every minute of every day. As Theodore Roosevelt said, "I care not what others think of what I do, but I care very much about what I think of what I do! That is character!"

Gene Klann, author and leadership development expert at the Centre for Creative Leadership (CCL) highlighted in his book, *Building Character: Strengthening the Heart of Good Leadership (2007)*, "When people have disappointment or mistrust in their leaders, they are, in fact, questioning leadership character. A leader's behaviour reflects what they stand for and what their core nature is." For character to find the spotlight it deserves, leaders need to illuminate it.

All of us have character, but the key is the depth of development of each facet of it that enables us to lead in a holistic way. Character is not a light switch that can be turned on and off. It has degrees and every situation presents a different experience and opportunity to learn and deepen character. In particular, and for better or for worse, character comes to the fore when we are managing a crisis. No one has a 'perfect' character and, given its development is a lifelong journey, we will rise to the occasion in some situations and disappoint ourselves and those around us in others.

Developing Leadership Character

If a leader behaves in positive and constructive ways, they can earn respect and create strong connections with others. Leaders can make a significant difference by demonstrating and developing their leadership character. Here are three ways to do that:

- **Focus on behaviour**

  Leadership character is about tangible behaviour, Klann explains. It is what leaders say and do, regardless of what inner qualities they may possess or thoughts they may cherish, that determines their reputation and good name. They can learn how to speak and act in ways that reflect qualities such as courage, caring, self-control, optimism and effective communication.

- **Adjust, don't overhaul**

  Changing behaviour is not always easy. However, most people can see when there is an advantage to changing certain behaviour and can take action. Typically, adults change their behaviour to gain something positive or avoid something negative. The key is to go about change slowly in terms of adjusting behaviour, rather than expecting instant change.

- **Be consistent**

  Klann explains that a leader's reputation is based on their behaviour. When a leader's pattern of behaviour consistently reflects strong character, the result is greater respect, trust and stronger emotional connections between leaders and their employees.

The Case For Character In Leaders
Leaders With Character:

- **Achieve peace of mind**. They take great pride in knowing their intentions and actions are honourable.

Leaders with character also stay true to their beliefs, do right by others and always take the high ground.

- **Strengthen trust.** People with character enjoy meaningful relationships based on openness, honesty and mutual respect. When you have good moral character, people know your behaviour is reliable, your heart is in the right place and your word is good.
- **Build a solid reputation.** This helps them attract exciting opportunities.
- **Reduce anxiety and carry less baggage**. They are comfortable with themselves and accept responsibility for their actions. They never have to play games, waste precious time keeping their stories straight, or invent excuses to cover their behinds.
- **Increase leadership effectiveness.** They have no need to pull rank or resort to command and control to get results. Instead, they are effective because they are knowledgeable, admired, trusted and respected. This helps them secure buy-in automatically, without requiring onerous rules or strong oversight designed to force compliance.
- **Build confidence.** People with character don't worry about embarrassment if their actions are publicly disclosed. This alleviates the need for damage control or the fear of potential disgrace as a result of indiscretions.
- **Are positive role models.** They live their lives as an open book, teaching others important life lessons through their words and deeds.

Point In Action
Johnson & Johnson (J&J), US

Not surprisingly, the importance of leadership character is making inroads in the business world. Johnson & Johnson (J&J), the major manufacturer of healthcare products in the United States, views character as a leadership essential. Former chairman Ralph Larsen believes that people with character can give a company a significant competitive advantage. J&J actively seeks to recruit and be represented by people of exceptional character. Its stance is supported by research suggesting that in leadership, good character counts. According to Frances Hesselbein, the author and chairman of the Drucker Foundation, leadership that achieves results goes beyond how to be, and becomes how to do; this type of leadership is all about character. So in other words, to get things done personally and organisationally, we first need to get in touch with our character.

Leaders with character achieve results that transcend everyday organisational imperatives and outcomes. A study of world leaders over the past 150 years asserts that managers who possess strong character will create a better world for everyone, while leadership generally is vital to the social, moral, economic and political fabric of society.

Telecom NZ

Another example, Theresa Gattung, is the CEO of Telecom NZ, a New Zealand telecommunications company. Her candour about her vulnerabilities and her philosophy on leadership has won her the admiration of her colleagues. She recognises that good leadership consists more of character than personality:

"When I went to management school 20 years ago, I thought it was about personality, desire, determination and a little bit of technique. I didn't actually realise it was about character, and that struck me more as I have gone along... The leaders whom people respect and will follow have the characteristics of being themselves, of being passionate about what they are doing, communicating that in a heartfelt way that touches hearts."

Reflective Questions

1. What ethical or moral issues do you anticipate encountering in your leadership role? How well prepared are you for dealing with these issues?
2. What are your core beliefs? How do your actions back up those beliefs?
3. How do you lead from your core values? What changes can you make to lead more consistently from those values?
4. What are you passionate about? What are you doing to incorporate this into your role as a leader?

Chapter 10: Resilience

> *"Success is not final, failure is not fatal:*
> *it is the courage to continue that counts."*
> **Winston Churchill**

> *"Resilience is all about being able*
> *to overcome the unexpected. Sustainability*
> *is about survival. The goal is to thrive."*
> **Jamais Cascio**

What Is Resilience?

Simply defined, resilience is the ability to respond effectively to disruptive events. The belief that leaders have the endless stamina, ideas and skills required to deliver success year after year is a fallacy. Thus, resilience, the ability to bounce back, cope, renew and revitalise, has become a key watchword for today's savvy leaders. Being resilient means that when we do fail we bounce back, we have the strength to learn the lessons we need to learn and can move on to bigger and better things.

In his book *Resilience: hard-won wisdom for a better living* (2015), Eric Greitens highlights that success is seldom a straight road; it involves many detours and dead ends. It takes tenacity and determination to keep going, but those that do will eventually reach their destination. The true test of how far you have progressed on your leadership journey is how you handle adversity. Leaders who lead from within are resilient. They are not successful in spite of their setbacks; they are successful because of them.

> *The belief that leaders have the endless stamina, ideas and skills it takes to deliver success year after year is a fallacy*

How we view adversity and stress strongly affects how we succeed; this is one of the reasons why a resilient mindset is so important. The fact is, you are going to fail from time to time: it's an inevitable part of living that you make mistakes and occasionally fall flat on your face. The only way to avoid this is to live a shuttered and meagre existence, never trying anything new or taking risks. Few of us want a life like that. Instead, we should have the courage to go after our dreams, despite the very real risk that we will fail in one way or another.

The Importance Of Resilience

Resilient leaders do not wallow or dwell on failures; they acknowledge the situation, learn from their mistakes, then move forward. According to the research of leading psychologist, Jonathan Smith, in his book *Leadership resilience* (2013), there are three elements that are essential to resilience:

1. **Challenge** — Resilient leaders view a difficulty as a challenge, not a paralysing event. They look at their failures and mistakes as lessons to be learned and opportunities for growth. They don't view them as a negative reflection on their abilities or self-worth.

2. **Commitment** — Resilient leaders are committed to their lives and their goals, and they have a compelling reason to get out of bed in the morning. Commitment isn't just restricted to their work — they commit to their relationships, their friendships, the causes they care about and their religious or spiritual beliefs.

3. **Personal control** — Resilient leaders spend their time and energy focusing on situations and events that they can control. Because they put their efforts where they can have the most impact, they feel empowered and confident. Those who spend time worrying about uncontrollable events can often feel lost, helpless and powerless to take action.

Common Characteristics Of Resilient Leaders

1. **A positive image of the future.** Resilient leaders effectively identify opportunities in turbulent environments and have the personal confidence to believe they can succeed. When things don't go

according to plan, resilient leaders look for the learning in the situation and the lesson they can take away.

2. **A clear vision of what they want to achieve.** They use this as a road map to guide them when they become disoriented.

3. **A long-term view**, despite not seeing any immediate results of their efforts. They are keen and aware that their future will be determined by their efforts today. Their strong sense of the future motivates them to take action even when they see no immediate benefit and don't feel motivated in the moment.

4. **Empathy and compassion**. However, they don't waste time worrying about what others think of them. They maintain healthy relationships, but don't bow to peer pressure.

5. **Never think of themselves as victims**; they focus their time and energy on changing the things they have control over.

6. **Flexiblity** and drawing effectively on a wide range of internal and external resources to develop creative, pliable strategies for responding to change.

7. **They aren't frightened by uncomfortable thoughts** or not having the answers. They believe they will find a way.

8. **Find healthy ways to recharge and nurture** themselves. Resilient leaders are no less susceptible to pressures and life's stresses than anyone else, but

they have healthy coping mechanisms that they know they can count on.

Developing Resilience

Learning to be resilient is a full-time job that never stops. Unfortunately, there is no 'Resiliency 101' business-programme class. Families, schools, business and life give us many opportunities to continually develop coping skills and resilience.

If you are to enjoy continued success as a leader, you must understand two related issues on resilience. First, passion for excellence can take you only so far; you will burn out if you ignore your physical, emotional and mental limitations. The good news is that even if you are not a naturally resilient person, you can learn to develop a resilient mindset and attitude. So, what can you do differently to increase your capacity to lead with resilience?

Point In Action
From Bend, Not Break (2012) By Ping Fu

Imagine being torn out of your loving mother's arms at the age of eight. The next thing you know, you're alone, crammed on a train full of people headed for another city — one you barely know. You think that at least your aunt and uncle, whom you've met a handful of times before, will be waiting for you on your arrival.

But instead, you're greeted only by a couple of threatening teenagers in uniform who drop you off at a dormitory, where you join a ragtag group of other lost children. When you set foot in the small, dirty room that will be your home for the next ten years, you discover your four-year-old sister lying on the bare concrete floor, sobbing. She desperately needs your tender care.

In one day, you've not only lost your mother, you've become one yourself.

This is no nightmare. It is just "one small part "of the true story of Ping Fu, told in her memoir, *Bend, not break*.

Ping Fu's journey only grows more remarkable from that traumatic outset. She went on to face ten years of near-starvation, abuse and child labour as a factory worker and soldier during the Cultural Revolution in China. She received no formal education during that time.

But Ping never let these bitter experiences defeat her. On the contrary, she found beauty in nature and kindness in small acts of generosity from friends and neighbours. She refused to grow hard, but instead opened herself to compassion for all humankind, living the philosophy, 'Always err on the side of generosity'.

After arriving in the United States at the age of 25 with only $80 and a few words of English, Ping Fu worked her way through school as a computer programmer. She has since triumphed as founder and CEO of Geomagic, a software company that is leading the 3D printing and imaging revolution. In 2005, Ping Fu was named *Inc.* magazine's entrepreneur of the year. Today, she sits on US President Obama's Council on Innovation and Entrepreneurship. Above all, Ping Fu is one of the most generous, compassionate, and wise people I've ever had the honour to know.

Reflection Questions

1. How do you deal with the very real presence of ambiguity and complexity inherent in your world/life?
2. To what extent do you accept the reality that adversity is both inevitable and generally unexpected?
3. How can you continue to work positively within the unavoidable constraints imposed by the reality of the adverse circumstances?
4. What do you need to do to have positive influence and make good things happen in bad situations?

Section 2:
Leading through Others

L eadership has everything to do with relationships, the role of which cannot be overstated. If you want to know the effectiveness of a leader, ask those they lead. This is because there is no perfect assessment, no bright-line test for what makes a leader effective, and no model that can perfectly determine great leadership. Leadership is inherently a relational, communal process. Margaret Wheatley gives the following definiation in her book, Leadership Science (2012), "Leadership is always dependent on the context, but the context is established by the relationships we value."

Relationships are the connective tissue of an organisation. Over time, new relationships, built on trust and integrity, become the glue that holds us together.

Do you know leaders who excelled in one environment but failed elsewhere? How about leaders who were average in one organisation but spectacular in another? In my quest to explore this, I came to appreciate the importance of working through others. This section will explore leadership aspects such as:

1. presence;
2. relationship building; and
3. understanding power and its various manifestations.

We will look at each aspect of leading through others in the next few chapters.

Chapter 11:
Leadership Presence

"Absence sharpens love, presence strengthens it."
Thomas Fuller

*"As we let our light shine, we unconsciously give other
people permission to do the same. As we are liberated
from our fear, our presence actually liberates others."*
Marianne Williamson

What Is Presence?

People have a *de facto* style based on their personality
type, communication preferences and their own
aspirations and intentions. Yet the 'leadership presence'
of a person is defined by how others experience that
leadership. There's a myth that leadership presence is
innate — you either have it or you don't. While it is true
that leadership presence comes more naturally for some
than for others, the reality is that everyone can work on
developing a leadership presence. And once you achieve

this, it changes your frame of reference about who you are and the potential power you have to affect others positively.

So, presence is not an act or an image. It's not window dressing; it's not a charm offensive; it's not about power over others; and it's not necessarily about title, seniority or age. And it's definitely not trying to be somebody else. (Although observing others and learning from them can always help us be our best; in fact, I highly recommend doing just that.) One way to look at it is to think about being our best 'real' selves.

We've all come across leaders with presence.

Leaders with presence are comfortable with who they are. That's not the same as saying 'that's just the way I am and I can't change'. Leaders with presence are willing to hear feedback and improve in the areas that will make a positive difference to their leadership.

Leaders with presence are self-confident but not arrogant. They can be at their most powerful and 'present' when they are silent (listening), not just when they are in the spotlight. In fact, leaders with presence can help others to shine. They often have a strong personal 'brand.' We know what they stand for. They may have charisma, but leaders with charisma may not necessarily have presence. According to Jonno Hanafin, organisational development expert and author of *Use of self in OD consulting: what matters is presence (2007)*, "everyone possesses presence, regardless of the level of awareness of the impact of that presence. Presence is your distinctive use of self with intent by using yourself in the most powerful way. To be an effective leader, focusing on a continuous process of learning about one's conscious and unconscious reactions in different settings with different people is of paramount importance."

Why Leadership Presence?

Leadership presence, based on authenticity, is a powerful part of your leadership toolkit because it gets people to pay attention and respect you. It gives you an edge to help you grow your relationships with others. Leadership presence is the ability to do two things very well:

1. **Demonstrate your value,** whether to one person or to hundreds of thousands of people, in an authentic way.
2. **Connect well with your stakeholders.** It means being authentic, comfortable in your skin, and getting your message across while connecting with those around you. It is about connecting to your environment and current reality.

Presence is not a state, it's a process. It's about broadening your repertoire. Most leaders become successful based on their technical skills, but they need to recognise that leadership is not just about that. Soft-skill capabilities are particularly important. You need to think about three aspects of your leadership presence:

- the assumptions you bring to every situation;
- the communication skills you use; and
- the physical aspects of your presence.

Perceived Weirdness Index (PWI)

Jonno Hanafin developed the construct known as Perceived Weirdness index (PWI) in 1976. According to Hanafin, as a leader you need to be different enough to model and add value, but not so different to be repelled by the people you are trying to influence. What makes you successful in one situation isn't necessarily what will make you successful in the next. Managing PWI requires awareness, intent and timing.

At the beginning of a new engagement, the leader must be seen as similar enough to establish credibility. This comes from demonstrating familiarity with the situation, understanding the corporate terminology and having a comfortable but relaxed demeanour. It serves the leader well to emphasise being on the same wavelength as their 'followers' by expressing appreciation of their situation. Asking informed questions, offering examples and affirming your followers' perspectives are very important.

Cultivating Presence

In 2015 I graduated with a certificate in International Gestalt and Leadership Development (IGOLD), a programme with participants from 15 different countries. My tutors on the programme were John Nkrum, Dr. Mary Ann Rainey, Chantelle Wyley and Jonno Hanafin. According to these tutors, even though presence can't be manufactured, it can be cultivated. Cultivating presence requires more than knowing the latest management development models or attending conferences and workshops. These things are necessary but insufficient. Cultivating presence is a lifelong process.

1. **Work on your conversation skills.** Think about the last few times you talked to other people. How do you think they felt in your presence? Did you read their body language? When they walked away, do you think they felt better about themselves, or worse? Did they feel important in your presence? Did they feel listened to and engaged? Individuals who have leadership presence are able to put people at ease.

2. **Be authentic.** It can't be stressed enough that leadership presence is an inside-out job. There are more details in the previous chapter on authenticity.

3. **Show warmth.** Some people adopt a professional and crisp persona, hiding their genuine warmth to appear more executive. They have a formal approach to their relationships, but this is the opposite of what

executive presence is. People who have presence are approachable and engaging, whether they're dealing with a receptionist or a CEO. They're natural, exude warmth and show a genuine interest in those around them.

4. **Be present.** It's a misnomer that presence is about commanding a room — nothing could be further from the truth. Doing that means you want to be the centre of attention and metaphorically suck the oxygen out of a room. True presence is a focus on others.

5. **Assumptions.** Know yours! Assumptions that you hold dear can propel you to greatness or hold you back, but without being aware of what they are, you will never know how they are acting for you. Your beliefs are important because they permeate every interaction. Therefore, you have to condition these assumptions, keeping those that work and discarding the negative ones that pull you down. Three critical assumptions that every leader should examine are:

- **confidence**: what you bring to a situation;
- **perspective**: what role you have;
- **clarity**: what your values are.

Framed in a positive and collaborative fashion, these assumptions can help enhance your leadership presence.

Point In Action

Bill Clinton knows how to win friends and influence people. So what's his secret? It's simple: he gives everyone he meets his full, undivided attention. Paying attention may sound easy enough, but few of us apply our full focus when interacting with others. In our culture of distraction and multi-tasking, where digital devices vie with actual flesh-and-blood humans for our attention, the ability to engage completely with another person is an unusual trait. Clinton's mastery of the art of paying attention seems impressive and rare.

Our own lack of attention may be part of what makes Clinton's presence remarkable. A 2010 Harvard study found that we spend 47% of our waking hours thinking about something other than what we're doing. But countless anecdotes about Clinton suggest that his legendary charisma stems from the undivided attention he gives to every person he meets.

During a 1992 presidential debate, Clinton and George H.W. Bush were asked how the national debt affected them personally. The way the two politicians answered provided a great insight into their personalities. While Bush twisted the question to take the focus off himself, before muttering his way through an explanation of how price hikes affect everyone, Clinton walked over to the woman who asked the question, looked her in the eye, and asked her how the debt affected her. He explained how, as the Governor of

Arkansas, he'd seen the people in his state suffer, and how much of an impact it had on him.

"In my state, when people lose their jobs, there's a good chance I'll know them by name," Clinton said.

As a politician, Clinton understood the difference between talking 'at' people and talking 'to' or 'with' them. The Guardian's Alastair Campbell called Clinton "the greatest political communicator I ever saw". Paying attention was, and is, his secret weapon.

People can tell when you're actually listening to them, and they love it. It seems simple and obvious, but Clinton built a career on doing what most politicians can't or won't do: connecting with ordinary people, looking them in the eye and listening to what they have to say. His ability to listen was instrumental in his ability to win people over. "All my life I've been interested in other people's stories", Clinton wrote in *My Life (2004)*, "I wanted to know them, understand them, feel them".

Another thing Clinton did really well was eye contact. *Psychology Today* calls eye contact the "strongest form of nonverbal communication". And according to a University of Miami study (2013), over 43% of the attention we focus on someone is devoted to their eyes. Clinton's intense eye contact is a powerful display of his attention, and in some cases, it has elicited particularly strong reactions.

Reflection Questions

1. What assumptions do you hold about leadership presence?

2. What are some of the daily practices you need to cultivate your leadership presence?

3. What do you typically pay attention to? How does this affect your presence?

4. How do people feel after interacting with you?

Chapter 12:
Focus on Relationships

"Relationship skills are the most important ability in leadership."
John Maxwell

The most important single ingredient in the formula of success is knowing how to get along with people."
Theodore Roosevelt

Wouldn't it be wonderful to walk into a leadership position and lead the charge towards efficiency, effectiveness and higher profits and production without establishing and maintaining relationships with others? I don't think so! It's quite evident that an essential part of leading others is building and maintaining relationships with everyone in your organisation, at every level.

Effective leaders recognise the importance of building solid relationships. They spend time focusing their efforts on key areas that will build connections with the people they lead. Building relationships is one of the strongest skill sets related to leadership effectiveness according to Jean Leslie, a researcher at the Centre for Creative Leadership (CCL; www.ccl.org). Leaders with experience in building relationships are seen as more effective. The trouble is that today's leaders are not adept at building relationships, according to CCL. Relationship building ranked tenth out of 16 leadership competencies; meanwhile, only 47% of managers believed that "leaders in their organisations were highly skilled in collaboration". (Jean Lesley 2014).

Strong leadership does not negate the need for relationships; it embraces them. By themselves, leaders achieve very little; the measure of effective leadership lies in the results a leader achieves by inspiring others. In a corporate setting, those results come by working with people, either as individuals or as teams.

A relationship-driven leader empowers others and considers empathy essential to creating strong, productive teams. This type of leader also views decision making through a relationship-focused lens rather than a power- or title-based perspective.

Cultivating Your Relationship Building Skills

1. **Learn to read people**. Getting to know someone can occur more swiftly and genuinely over a shared meal, even in the corporate cafeteria. When you sit

across someone you can listen as you munch; you can observe the person and make mental notes about what they say, or likely do not say. In time, you can determine motivation and aspiration as well as commitment.

2. **Do unto others as you would have them do unto you**. Yup, it's a golden rule and believe it or not, it works in leadership too. Relationships emerge from trust; you establish trust by personal example.

3. **Put yourself out there**. If you want to collaborate, you need to get more involved in new things. Genuine collaboration calls for the blending of ideas, a synthesis that creates a better whole.

4. **Listen and let other people talk.** Pay attention to what other people are saying. Remove anything that could distract you from conversations and focus on what people are trying to convey.

5. **Understand.** In addition to being open to ideas, be eager and open to learning new things. Taking the time to understand where people are coming from will pay dividends in the long run.

6. **Acknowledge** the contributions of others. Be quick to give credit to others for their successes. Celebrate achievements and delight in the accomplishments of your team.

7. **Coach and develop others' ability to create value.** Another way to deepen relationships also happens to be a critical responsibility for most leaders.

Reflection Questions

1. To what extent are you intentional about building relationships with your "followers"?
2. What else can you do to be more intentional about building these relationships?
3. How can you hone your listening skills?

Chapter 13:
Taking The Time To Get To Know Others

*"Knowing others is intelligence; knowing
yourself is true wisdom. Mastering others is strength;
mastering yourself is true power. If you realise that
you have enough, you are truly rich."*
Lao Tzu, Tao Te Ching

People generally have some level of care and concern for those they work with. Expressing that professionally will help you relate to others. We each have unique emotions attached to what makes us feel appreciated. According to Gary Chapman, author of *The five love languages* (2009), our motivation is maximised when we receive our ideal form of praise, encouragement or reward for our efforts. Asking questions about the impact of something and focusing intently on the answer is one of your best methods for developing high-quality relationships.

As a leader, there are so many ways of building effective personal and professional relationships with people. One is through understanding your love language (yes, you read that correctly!) and that of those you work with.

According to Chapman, being loved is our deepest human desire. It is often left unmet due to differences in the way we express and receive love. He explains that for us to meet this deep-seated need, the love we receive must make sense to us.

Based on Chapman's original book and understanding of love languages, Dr. White saw the need for the love languages in the workplace. "Every person is unique in the way that they feel love or express love in personal relationships, but it's the same in how they feel appreciated and valued in work relationships," explain Chapman and White (Author and Leadership expert).

Thus, *The 5 languages of appreciation in the workplace: empowering, organizations by encouraging people* (2015) was born. The five emotional languages Chapman describes are:

1. Words of affirmation: use words to affirm people
2. Acts of service: actions speak louder than words
3. Giving and receiving gifts: people like to be given things to feel appreciated
4. Quality time: giving someone undivided attention
5. Physical touch: appropriate touch (pats on the back)

Chapman and White contend that individuals speak and understand different emotional languages. They hold different opinions about how to communicate their love and, in turn, what makes them feel loved. The following questions may give some clues about a person's primary language:

- How do you express love to others?
- What do you request most often?
- What do you complain about? What do others do to show their love to you?

Consider if an individual takes time to do things for someone else. Once a leader learns the primary languages of individuals, they can focus on speaking the preferred language using some of the following suggestions:

Appreciation Languages
Acts Of Service

Your followers whose appreciation language is 'acts of service' will naturally show this by doing things for others. You will see them going out of their way to help other team members. 'Acts of service' people are great to have on your team. They are the nurturers. Making an effort to help these people will massively boost their loyalty to you. Do something nice for them; they will see that you care. Doing something as simple as helping your teammate out with a solo project or task will communicate immense value. I've known others who would rather die than be singled out for anything. Instead, these people thrive when someone offers to help them finish a task, when a colleague backs them up in a project, when their boss rolls up their sleeves to help clear the backlog. This breeds undying loyalty.

Physical Touch

The people with 'physical touch' are easy to figure out. They always love to give hugs, place their hands on your shoulders or shake hands. One effective way to communicate your appreciation is to give high fives during times of recognition. Or just give them a high five (or a hug if you're close) on a regular basis. I promise they won't complain. One thing I have noticed about team members with this love language is that they are the physical motivators. They get people 'amped up' with their high fives of power and motivation. To encourage physical touch is a little difficult as, taken literally, it could land you in hot water. However, if you think about it, it's to do with intimacy. This means one-on-one time with this individual would go down a treat. So, create opportunities for a weekly chat over coffee, ask about their family and tell them about yours, take them to visit a client with you or have a brainstorming session. This will boost their self-esteem and build lasting bonds.

Quality Time

This language may be a little more difficult to spot as, in my experience, most 'quality timers' do not directly communicate this need. You will have to learn and listen to this specific love language. When you are having a team meeting involving someone you suspect is a 'quality timer', ask to speak to them personally. When this happens, ask them what they thought about the meeting, what could be done to improve productivity and so on. Be sure to tell them they have your undivided attention. If you see their eyes light up, you have a winner! Support would be meaningless to someone who thrives on continual development. Being nominated to go on a development programme, being selected to attend a global training course, being given access to new tools, trends or being enabled to complete a degree will make this individual feel on top of the world. People who prefer this indicator of love want to share experience and communicate closely with others. To meet this need, it is important to consider opportunities to share time while being fully present. During this time, listen for emotions being expressed, put away your mobile phone and other gadgets and just 'be'. You can involve others in projects or simply take the time to ask questions about work, family or hobbies and genuinely listen to the reply.

Giving And Receiving Gifts

People who speak this language will benefit most from rewards of recognition, which are most effective when given publicly. When your teammate reaches a milestone in their career or your coaching client hits a new goal, give them something to remind them of their achievement. It could be a seven-day cruise to Alaska or a printed certificate of completion. It doesn't even have to be for something huge. If you see them do something you like, tell them! "Hey, I really appreciate how you stepped up back there" or "that was really brave of you to speak up in the meeting". Not all gifts are physical. This individual may think spending one-on-one time with the boss is like watching paint dry; however, putting a prize up for grabs, dropping a gift on their desk, giving them a phenomenal stretch bonus will make this colleague take off like a rocket.

Words Of Affirmation

Those with this love language are the easiest to spot. All you have to do is listen. Which of your team members are constantly encouraging and lifting up others? Who is always complimenting people? I personally think this is the easiest language to please. If you're good at listening and observing what's going on, then you will have no problem at communicating value to other people.

Show them you're paying attention. Compliment them on their well-kept appearance (just don't go overboard). Say something nice about their hard work and perseverance. Affirm their strengths and remind them why they're going to succeed.

I've worked with many individuals who thrive in the limelight. Being singled out for specific achievements (no matter how small), words of praise and even blatant flattery can put a spring in someone's step. People who thrive on affirmation want to hear and know that others love and appreciate them. For these individuals, affirmation is often more valuable than financial reward. Leaders can make special efforts to recognise what individuals do and thank them personally or in writing. They can be sure to recognise them publicly as they also realise that some individuals do not want that.

These are all behaviours that leaders should cultivate, but being aware of a person's preference helps to strengthen relationships by focusing on the things that matter most to people. This attitude requires a willingness to give. It also requires leaders to be sensitive and emotionally intelligent to adjust when they go too far. However, learning a person's primary emotional language and using it to bond relationships is valuable and worthwhile.

Reflection Questions

1. Do you have the ability to relate to people?

2. How do you react, both consciously and unconsciously, to people with different backgrounds, communication styles or ideas?
3. How do you initiate building relationships? Start by looking in unlikely places.

Chapter 14:
Leadership and Power

"If a man can accept a situation in a place of power with the thought that it's only temporary, he comes out all right. But when he thinks that he is the cause of the power; that can be his ruination."
Harry S. Truman

What Is Power?

We cannot talk about leading from within and leading with others without talking about power. What comes to mind when you think of the term? Does it elicit positive or negative feelings?

The influence of a leader over his followers is often referred to as power. Power extends far beyond the formal authority that comes from a title (or from having a corner office with a view). I asked a number of my friends what they thought when they heard the word, and most of them said their minds go immediately to the control that high-level leaders exert from their positions at the top of organisational hierarchies. Leaders at all levels have access to power; often that power goes unrecognised or underutilised.

Knowing the sources and types of power is important for every leader who wants to lead with integrity and from an authentic perspective.

Types Of Power

Legitimate power is a person's ability to influence others' behaviour because of the position they hold within an organisation or group, such as a family. Legitimate, or position power as it is sometimes called, is derived from a position of authority inside an organisation, often referred to as 'formal authority'. That is, the organisation has given to an individual the right to influence and direct other individuals. When a manager asks an employee to work late to complete a project or work on one task instead of another, they are exercising legitimate power.

Managers can enhance their position power by formulating policies and procedures. For example, they might establish a requirement that all new hires must be approved by a designated manager, thus exercising authority over hiring.

Subordinates play a major role in the exercise of legitimate power. If they view the use of power as legitimate, they comply. That is, legitimate power covers a relatively narrow range of influence and, therefore, it may be inappropriate to overstep these boundaries. For example, a boss may require their secretary to type a company document. However, it would be an abuse of power to ask that secretary to type the boss's doctoral dissertation. The secretary may decide to complete the task, but doing so would not be within the scope of the boss's formal authority.

Legitimate power can be depended on initially, but continued reliance on it may create dissatisfaction, resistance, and frustration among employees. If legitimate power does not coincide with expert power, there may be negative effects on productivity; and dependence on legitimate power may lead to only minimum compliance while increasing resistance.

Reward power is a person's ability to influence others' behaviour by providing them with things they want. These rewards can be either financial, such as pay rises or bonuses, or non-financial, such as promotions, favourable work assignments, more responsibility, new equipment, praise and recognition. A manager can use reward power to influence and control employees' behaviour, as long as employees value the rewards. For example, if you offer employees what you think are rewards (e.g. a promotion with more responsibility) but your employees do not value them (e.g. they are insecure or they prioritise family obligations), then you really do not have reward power as a manager and leader.

Reward power can lead to better performance, as long as the employee sees a clear link between performance and rewards. To use reward power effectively, you should be explicit about the behaviour being rewarded and should make clear the connection between the behaviour and the reward.

Coercive power is a person's ability to influence others' behaviour by punishing them or creating a perceived threat to do so. For example, employees may comply with a manager's directive because of fear or threat of punishment. Typical organisational punishments include reprimands, undesirable work assignments, withholding key information, demotion, suspension or dismissal.

Coercive power has negative side effects and should be used with caution, because it tends to result in negative feelings toward those who use it. The availability of coercive power varies from one organisation and manager to another. Most organisations have clearly defined policies on employee treatment. Clear rules and procedures that govern how coercive power is used prevent superiors from using their legitimate power (formal authority) arbitrarily and unethically. The presence of unions can also weaken coercive power considerably.

You do not need to be in a position of authority to possess coercive power. Employees also have coercive power, including the use of sarcasm and fear of rejection to ensure that team members conform to group norms. Many organisations rely on the coercive power of team members to control employee behaviour. Although coercive power may lead to temporary compliance by subordinates, it produces the undesirable side effects of frustration, fear, revenge and alienation. This, in turn, may lead to poor performance, dissatisfaction and higher staff turnover.

Expert power is a person's ability to influence others' behaviour because of recognised knowledge, skills or abilities. Physicians are acknowledged to have expertise, special skills and knowledge and, hence, expert power. Most people follow their doctor's advice. Computer specialists, tax accountants and economists also have power because of their expertise.

Experts have power even when they rank low in an organisation's hierarchy. As organisations become increasingly more technologically complex and specialised, the expert power of an organisation's members at all levels in the hierarchy becomes more important. Some organisations deliberately include lower-level staff members with expert power in top-level decision making. Knowledge is power in today's high-tech workplaces.

Expert power is based on the extent to which followers attribute knowledge and expertise to the power holder. Experts are perceived to have expertise in well-defined functional areas but not outside them. To be granted expert power, followers must perceive the power holder to be credible, trustworthy, and relevant. Credibility is acquired by having the appropriate credentials. For example, physicians, computer specialists and tax accountants, who have shown tangible evidence of their expertise, will be listened to closely and thereby granted expert power. These specialists may not be granted expert power in other functional areas.

The person seeking expert power also must be trustworthy and have a reputation for being honest. In addition to credibility and trustworthiness, a person must have relevance. For example, if physicians gave advice on political issues it would not be relevant, and they would not have expert power.

Referent power is a person's ability to influence others' behaviour because they like, admire and respect the individual. For example, suppose you are friends with your boss. One day, she asks you to take on a special project that you do not like. With anyone else, you would probably decline the request, but because of your special relationship with this individual, you may do it as a favour. In this instance, your boss has power over you because of your positive relationship.

Referent power develops out of admiration for another and a desire to be like that person. This helps to explain why celebrities are paid millions of pounds in endorsements. Marketing research shows that sports people such as Usain Bolt and Serena Williams have the power to influence your choice of athletic shoes and tennis products, respectively. The same could be said of leaders in business firms who have a good reputation, attractive personal characteristics, or a certain level of charisma.

Referent power can lead to enthusiastic and unquestionable trust, compliance, loyalty and commitment from subordinates. Like expert power, much less surveillance of employees is required.

A true leader is able to influence others and modify behaviour via legitimate and referent power. It is possible for a leader to possess all sources of power at the same time. In fact, the most powerful leaders have sources that include all five forms.

Generally, personal sources of power are more strongly related to employees' job satisfaction, organisational commitment and performance than organisational power sources. One source of organisational power — coercive power — is negatively related to employee satisfaction, commitment and job performance.

Furthermore, the various sources of power are interrelated. For example, managers' use of coercive power may reduce their referent power, and the use of coercive and reward power may lead to reduced expert power.

Reflection Questions

1. Are you as powerful as you could be at work?
2. What sources of power are you good at using now, and what do you need to work on?
3. What do you do if your organisation gets in the way of you being as powerful as you could be?
4. What could you do for others to help them be more powerful?

Section 3: Leading from a Systemic Perspective

Chapter 15: Systemic Leadership

The complex world in which you are operating in bewildering uncertainty requires you to think systemically. Gone are the days when influencing your immediate environment was enough. Today's leadership challenges are rarely simple and clear cut. If they were, they would have been solved already. If not well considered, and sometimes even when they are, today's solutions become tomorrow's problems. Success in the contemporary operating environment requires different ways of thinking about problems and organisations. At the most fundamental level, this requires moving from a 'linear' way of thinking, where we focus on quickly fixing the most visibly broken parts of what isn't working, to a 'systems' perspective that brings thought and behaviour into line with the natural laws of sustainability.

What Is A System?

Systems, like the human body, have parts, which affect the performance of the whole. All parts are interdependent. The liver interacts with and affects other internal organs — the brain, heart, kidneys, etc. You can study the parts individually, but because of the interactions it doesn't make practical sense to stop there. Understanding the system cannot depend on analysis alone.

If you imagine your company as a living body, systems thinking makes a little more sense. Take your company's organisational chart and draw a line to someone. How would you describe your connection to them? If that person drew a line to someone else in the chart, how would they describe the connection? By noticing how each part of your organisation affects the others, you are engaging in basic systems thinking.

When there are breakdowns (missed deadlines, conflicts, customer complaints, etc.), it is easier to explore the issues and find a way to resolve or manage problems. As the leader, you can define how involved you get, share power more easily and be more focused on how you contribute to the system overall. This can support the overall business goals and nurture a positive work culture. Systems challenges are usually dilemmas to be managed rather than problems to be solved.

Characteristics Of Systems Leadership

The characteristics of systems leadership are different from those that have often succeeded within a single organisation or a limited project.

1. Systems leadership is almost the opposite of command and control, since in system change no-one can see the whole picture or know everything about how to make the change happen. It can't be outsourced or delegated since the energy and creativity needed has to work all the way up (and down).
2. Because change involves a group of leaders, rather than just one, it is not enough to have a powerful vision and simply charge ahead. It is important to take others with you, to create a shared endeavour and strong, trustworthy relationships.
3. Leaders are often working 'beyond the boundaries of their authority' in situations where they are no longer the boss but have to win consent from communities, partners and stakeholders, sometimes in situations that pose as risks to their reputations or careers. So, this sort of leadership always involves a choice.
4. The alternative to a linear top-down direction is not chaos, but a self-conscious and carefully planned set of interventions.

The Importance Of Networks

Networks are more important than structures. Meetings are not necessarily the places where leadership takes place. The ostensible leaders are not the only, or even the most important, leaders and the real work takes place in informal rather than formal settings. It is important to understand this, because many very busy senior people spend their lives racing between meetings without time to prepare or think in advance, and are then surprised when the meeting doesn't achieve anything.

Change Needs To Happen Everywhere In Parallel

One of the most useful pieces of learning from a system enabler is that change needs to begin everywhere, as parts of the system can go cold if it's too staged and sequential. People who were excited at the beginning may feel like their 'bit' of the system is not changing and that attention is focused elsewhere, so they drop out or lose interest.

What Do Systems Leaders Do?

- Go out of their way to make new connections.
- Adopt an open, enquiring mindset, refusing to be constrained by current horizons.
- Embrace uncertainty and be positive about change — adopt an entrepreneurial attitude.

- Draw on as many different perspectives as possible; diversity is not optional.
- Ensure leadership and decision making is distributed throughout all levels and functions.
- Establish a compelling vision that is shared by all partners in the whole system.
- Lead 'without authority', relying on influence rather than position.

Reflection Questions

1. As a leader, do you or your staff have sufficient knowledge of the outside world (competitor knowledge, etc.)? How do you keep the knowledge current?
2. How do you and your leadership team take interest in other parts of the organisation?
3. Are you a role model? Do you model collaboration, trade favours, share resources and exchange information?
4. Do you and your team understand the scale of operation across the organisation?
5. What type of diversity do you have within your workplace?
6. Within your current culture and mindset, how do you see diversity in thinking, in approaches to work, culture, ethnicity etc.?
7. What type of diversity do you currently have that will give you the edge?

Notes and Sources

Chapter 1: Self-awareness

Bradberry, T & Greaves, J (2003). The emotional intelligence quick book, New York, NY: Fireside Books

Hanson, P. (2000). The self as an instrument for change, Organization Development Journal, 18 (1) p 95 – 105

Seashore, C, Shawver, M, Tompson, G, and Mattare, M (2004). Doing good by knowing who you are: the instrumental self as an agent of change, OD Practitioner, 36 (3), p 55-60

Shayla R. Price S, (2012), Leading from within: Become the mindful leader, p 53-56

Chapter 2: Knowing Your purpose

Warrell M (year). Stop Playing Safe, MsGraw-Hill

Sinek S (2011). Start with Why: How Great Leaders Inspire Everyone to Take Action, Penguine Group

Chapter 3: Receiving feedback

Stone D, (2015), The feedback challenge, p 3-15

Seashore CN, (2013) What did you say? The art of giving and receiving feedback, Douglas Charles Press

Grimsley A, (2010) Vital conversations, Barnes Holland Publishing, p 173-175

Schmuckler J., Giving feedback to leaders: Avoid the traps, Harvard Business Review, Apr 2014

Chapter 4: Acknowledge your blind spots

Radcliffe S., (2012), Leadership Plain and simple, Pearson, 2nd edition

Luft J, The Johari Window: A graphic model of awareness in interpersonal relationships, NTL Reading Book for Human Relations Training, p 34-35

Tenbrusnel A, Bazerman M, (2011), Blind spots: Why we fail to do what's right and what to do about it, Princeton University Press

Folkman J, (2015), Top Leaders know this secret: Ask for feedback, Forbes.com

Chapter 5: Establish and work on your growth edges

Gerald A, (2010), Creating your personal growth plan, p 1-4

Gershon D, (2008), Increasing the performance capacity of societal institutions: growing leaders to grow people in organizations

Chapter 6: Personality preferences

www.myersbriggs.org

www.opp.com

Chapter 7: Leadership style

Burks A, (2011). Leadership Styles: Benefits, deficiencies and their influence on organisation,

Chapter 8: Authentic leadership

Mohr T, (2014), Playing big, Hutchinson London, p 8-10

Jones G, Goffee R, (2006), Why should anyone be led by you, p 109-112

George B, Sims P, Discovering your authentic leadership, Harvard Business Review, February 2007

Kruse K., What is authentic leadership, Forbes, May 2013 issue

George B, (2004), Authentic leadership: Rediscovering the secrets to creating lasting value, Warren Bennis

Chapter 9: Importance of Character

Crossan M, Gabdz J, Seijts G (2008). The cross-enterprise leader, Ivey Business Journal

Warren B, (1989). On becoming a leader, Random House Business Books

Klan G, (2007). Building Character: Strengthening the Heart of Good Leadership, John Wiley and Sons

Chapter 10: Resilience

Cashman K, (2010) Leadership from the inside out, p 128

Sander S, Why is resilience so hard, Harvard Business Review, November 2013

George PD, Everly G, (2010), The secrets of resilient leadership: when failure is not an option, DiaMedica Publishing

Sinek, S, (2011), Start with why: how great leaders inspire everyone to take action (p 236). Penguin Books Ltd, Kindle edition

Chapter 11: Leadership presence

Rainey Tolbert MA., Hanafin J, (2006), Use of self in OD consulting, what matters is presence, p 69-81

Hanafin, J, (1976), PWI: Perceived weirdness index (Educational document). Cleveland: Gestalt Institute of Cleveland

Wolman R, (2001), Thinking with your soul, New York Harmony Books

Chapter 12: Focus on relationships

Cashman K, (2010), Leadership from the inside out, p 32-40

Ladkin D, Leading beautifully: how mastery, congruence and purpose create the aesthetic of embodied leadership practice, The Leadership Quarterly, Volume 19, Issue 1, February 2008, p 31-41

Bass, BM, (1985), Leadership and performance beyond expectations, New, York: Free Press

Drath, W, (2001), The deep blue sea: Rethinking the source of leadership, San Francisco: Jossey-Bass

Chapter 13: Taking the time to know others

Chapman G., White P, (2012), The 5 languages of appreciation in the workplace: empowering organisations by encouraging people, (p 21-31)

Chapter 14: Leadership and power

Lunenburg FC, Power and leadership: an influence process, International Journal of Management, Business and Administration, Volume 15, Number 1, 2012

Green D, (1999), Leadership as a function of power, p 54-56

Bal V, Campbell M, (2008), The role of power in effective leadership, CCL Research White paper, 2008

Pfeffer J, (2010), Power: Why some people have it and others don't

Chapter 15: Systemic leadership

Scott P, Harris J, & Florek A, Systems leadership for effective services, Report no 2, 2013